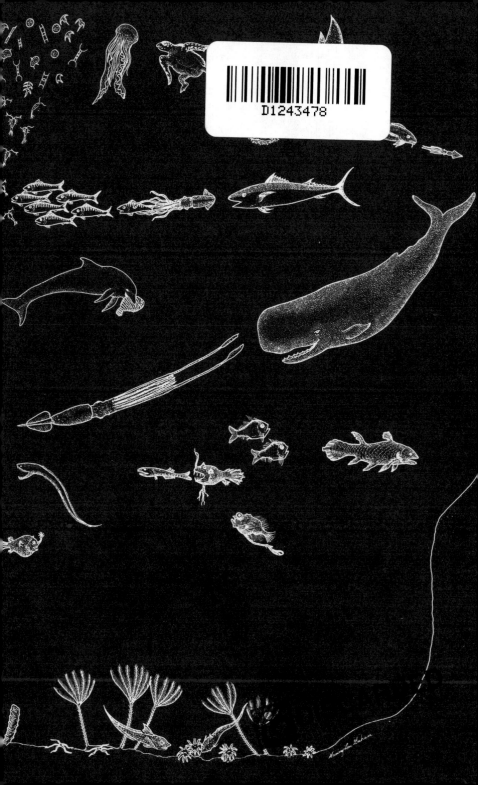

D1243478

THE UNKNOWN OCEAN

Other books by Richard Perry
THE WORLD OF THE TIGER
THE WORLD OF THE POLAR BEAR
THE WORLD OF THE WALRUS
THE WORLD OF THE GIANT PANDA
THE WORLD OF THE JAGUAR
AT THE TURN OF THE TIDE

QL
124
.P47
1972

THE
UNKNOWN OCEAN

Richard Perry

Illustrated by Nancy Lou Gahan

VOLUME I: THE MANY WORLDS OF WILDLIFE SERIES

Taplinger Publishing Company   *New York*

First published in the United States in 1972 by
TAPLINGER PUBLISHING CO., INC.
New York, New York

Copyright © 1972 by Richard Perry
Illustrations copyright © 1972 by Taplinger Publishing Co., Inc.
All rights reserved. Printed in the U.S.A.

No part of this publication may be reproduced or transmitted in any
form or by any means, electronic or mechanical, including photocopy,
recording, or any information storage and retrieval system now known
or to be invented, except by a reviewer who wishes to quote brief
passages in connection with a review written for inclusion in a
magazine, newspaper or broadcast.

Published simultaneously in the Dominion of Canada by
Burns & MacEachern Ltd., Ontario

Library of Congress Catalog Card Number: 71-148828

ISBN 0-8008-7938-4

For Brent
in the night watches

ACKNOWLEDGMENTS

To all those skin-divers and undersea explorers, marine biologists and mariners whose books and papers I have plundered in search of the elusive truth; to the staff of the Reference Department of the Morpeth branch of the Northumberland County Library; the Librarian of the Marine Biological Association of the United Kingdom; Lieutenant Dudley Pound RN; and the following authors and publishers for permission to quote from their books: *Inagua* by Gilbert Klingel (Robert Hale, 1942); *Diving to Adventure* by Hans Hass (Jarrolds, Hutchinson Publishing Group, 1952); A *Pattern of Islands* by Sir Arthur Grimble (John Murray, 1952); *The Living Sea* by Jacques-Yves Cousteau and James Dugan (Harper & Row, Publishers, Inc., 1963); *In the Wake of the Sea Serpents* by Bernard Heuvelmans (Hill & Wang, 1968); *Dolphins* by Anthony Alpers (Houghton Mifflin Company, 1961); and the Editor of *Animals*.

CONTENTS

ILLUSTRATIONS

Introduction

This is essentially a book of questions. The development of relatively simple underwater breathing equipment since World War II, together with limited use of bathyspheres, bathyscaphes, diving-saucers and temporarily inhabited undersea research stations, has made it possible for man to begin the exploration of the virtually unknown ocean deeps which cover two-thirds of the earth's surface. With an average depth of more than 12 miles, and of from 4 to 7 miles in the stupendous volcanic and seismic trenches, the ocean is an infinitely more fascinating and rewarding realm for exploration than the sterile moon and planets. The bizarre variety of its multitudinous life has been partially revealed by the strange harvests of fishermen, by chance encounters of mariners, and by the deep trawls of marine biologists. The latter, however, admit that much of the data they have amassed during their tens of thousands of hours of patient and difficult dredging, and their hundreds of thousands of hours of ingenious laboratory research, must be reworked, and their theories revised, in the new light of direct observation by the skin-diver's eye and the underwater camera.

It is fair to say that we still do not know the full life history of a single marine animal. Of the habits of those that live only a few hundred feet below the surface we know almost nothing. Indeed, it was only when I was three-quarters of the way through Pierre de Latil's account, in *The Underwater Naturalist*, of the experiences of the underwater fishermen of the French Riviera that it dawned on me that here was the first attempt to present a natural history of fish from direct observation, comparable to those of mammals and of birds to which we are accustomed.

Blind trawls and nets catch mainly the small slow-swimming creatures in midwater and on smooth bottoms. We now know that many even of these are never caught, for electronic flash-cameras show that some of them can swim at speeds of from 3 to 10 feet per second—swiftly enough to evade any net. Among reefs and on rocky bottoms, where so many fish and crustaceans live, trawl nets are torn, get lost or are in-effectual. Recent collections of reef fish obtained by divers working in depths of from 150 to 200 feet off the Bahamas have included the astounding proportion of nearly 40 per cent of previously unknown species. It is possible that over untrawled rocky bottoms beyond the reefs, at depths of 400 feet, three-quarters of the fish may still be unknown.

If this is true of one minute area of the sea's upper waters, what remains to be discovered in the deep waters lying beneath the ocean's 130 million square miles, and in the further 10 million miles of shallower waters over the continental shelves, which slope gently down from the fore-shore for distances varying from a score or two to several hundred miles and terminate abruptly, at a depth of 600 feet, in the steep cliffs, gashed with canyons and gullies, that plunge 18,000 feet to the ocean floor? The floor itself is riven by the great trenches, some of them 2,000 miles long. There is more than enough exploration and observation in this new world to occupy all sorts and conditions of men far beyond the close of this millennium. And if that in itself is not sufficient reward, there is the exciting possibility that the emotions and intellectual capabilities of some marine mammals may more nearly approach man's than do those of any land mammal.

This book is devoted to the creatures in the deep waters beyond the reefs and the continental shelves. What are the life histories of the inhabitants of this undersea world? How do they contend with the problems of their unique environment? What are their relationships one with another? In attempting to answer these questions I have found myself in a realm of half-knowledge where almost every statement is debatable, where it has often been difficult to find two authorities in agreement and estimates differ by millions from one source to another, and where new discoveries are not only constantly opening up fresh lines of research but bewilderingly undermining what were previously supposed to be hard facts. However, life without the excitement of discovery, whether at first hand or vicariously, would be unendurable.

RICHARD PERRY

Northumberland, 1972

THE UNKNOWN OCEAN

1: The Complex World of Plankton

Once living cells had been sparked into eternal activity, eons ago, in the tepid ooze of the shallow coastal seas, which seem to have contained all the requisite elements for life, evolution could not be halted. For these microscopic forms of life not only could subsist on such inorganic foods as phosphates and nitrates, but were also able to capture the infinitesimal amounts of sunlight penetrating the upper 300 feet of the sea and, through the agency of the green pigment chlorophyll and the process of photosynthesis, make use of this energy to convert carbon dioxide and water into organic carbohydrates such as suger and starches.

These organisms were early forms of plant life, the phytoplankton. Sooner or later, measured in terms of millions of years, it was inevitable that random assemblages of molecules would result in a different form of life, the zooplankton, which could convert the phytoplankton into food and also breathe the oxygen which the latter released into the sea.

But the distinctions between primitive forms of plant and animal are so slight that certain plankton, such as the dinoflagellates, cannot be definitely assigned to either category.

As in the beginning, so today the continued existence of all animal life in the ocean—whether zooplankton, sardine, flying fish, turtle, squid, 30-foot basking shark, 100-ton blue whale, seal or sea bird—is directly or indirectly dependent on the seasonal reproduction of the phytoplankton, which constitute nine-tenths of marine plant life and consist predominantly of diatoms, those single-celled algae housed in virtually indestructible siliceous shells of infinite variety and beauty, the largest only 1/50 inch long. These are the ocean's basic source of food, and the lives of all its inhabitants are geared to their seasonal proliferation and recession.

The world of the innumerable forms of plankton is as complex as the biologists' varying observations on it and theories about it; but it would seem true to say that in the spring the amount of sunlight penetrating the surface layers of temperate and polar seas increases daily, just when these layers have been fertilized with nitrates and phosphates stirred up from the colder deeps by winter storms. This combination of phenomena activates the phytoplankton to such astronomical reproductive multiplication that a single quart of sea water may contain two hundred thousand diatoms, and hundreds of miles of ocean are stained red or yellow, green or brown with multiplying algae.

The population explosion of the diatoms is followed almost immediately by a comparable multiplication of the zooplankton, which graze on these fresh spring pastures, and their multitudes are incalculably increased by the eggs and fry of fish rising from the spawning beds on the bottom of the shallow continental waters in order to feed on the plankton in the upper few hundred feet. The eggs of most of these fish are buoyant, kept afloat by droplets of oil; and it is probable that those of the fauna from the abysses of the ocean also float up into surface waters, developing as they ascend.

Ocean diatoms

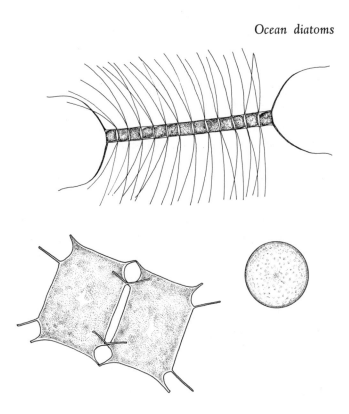

For example, although angler fish, which inhabit the depths between 3,000 and 12,000 feet, have never been caught at higher levels, their fry appear in the surface waters of the North Atlantic at definite seasons, in order to feed on the plankton, and do not descend into the abyss again until they have grown substantially; and while sea urchins are found as deep as 16,000 feet, their eggs could not develop at such a depth because under abyssal pressures the protoplasm in them would congeal like the white of a hard-boiled egg.

The planktonic explosion is most dramatic in the Antarctic, during the short summer from December to March, when the cold surface waters are displaced by a warmer current carrying nutrient salts. The resulting multiplication of diatoms triggers off a comparable explosion of predators in the form of shrimplike crustaceans, the euphausiids—or krill, as they are known to whalers. Their concentrations at the edge of the ice pack are so vast that one may cover more than 3,500 square miles, and so dense that immense areas of surface waters are transformed into a reddish-brown soup thick enough to slow a ship to half-speed.

In temperate and polar waters the vernal explosion of the phytoplankton wanes in a matter of weeks, as they exhaust the supplies of phosphates and nitrates. These cannot be adequately replaced from deeper and colder waters because during the summer the sun-heated upper 60 feet or so of the ocean becomes a few degrees warmer, and the thermocline or demarcation between that and the colder lower layer is sharply defined. The difference in density prevents any extensive inter-mingling of the two layers. By midsummer photosynthesis has virtually ceased, and the zooplankton have also finished spawning. However, in the late summer and autumn the surface waters cool again and storm waves upset the density barrier. The resultant refertilizing of upper waters stimulates a resurgence of the diatoms and various forms of zooplankton, which graze upon them, but the decline in photosynthesis, as the daily amount of sunlight decreases, limits the extent and duration of this resurgence.

In tropical seas the plankton reproduce throughout the year, but their total mass does not compare with that produced by the seasonal proliferation in the nutritious waters of colder latitudes. Since the surface waters in the tropics are perennially warm and reach temperatures as high as 95 degrees F. in the Red Sea and the Persian Gulf, the barrier of the thermocline is more or less permanent. At 400 feet in the Red Sea, Cousteau's diving saucer stopped sinking and rested on this invisible paper-thin thermocline until it had cooled off to a temperature of 73 degrees F. At the equator the thermocline is 750 feet down, and in the tropics at twice that depth. These, therefore, are the main levels of marine activity in warmer seas, and the hunting grounds of predatory fish, squids and prawns. The surface waters are correspondingly less populous and do not attract the great concentrations of predatory seals and sea birds that frequent the northern and southern oceans. When the seas among the Falkland Islands are stained pink by the concentrations of the shrimplike krill, feeding on lesser plankton brought to the surface by the fierce tide-rips, the flights of sea birds to and from these waters are almost unbroken for days at a time. Their feeding flocks may cover areas of sea more than a mile square, for four million blackbrowed albatrosses breed in the Falklands, and as many more penguins, petrels and shearwaters.

But the richest of all the ocean waters are probably those of the Humboldt Current, which conveys a cold stream of deep water northward off Peru to the region of the equator, where it is met by a warm countercurrent, El Niño, which brings water of low salinity from the tropics. Since the prevailing southeast trade winds blow the warm surface waters away from the Peruvian coast, the deep waters of the Humboldt Current are able to rise, carrying with them superabundant supplies of chemical and mineral nutrients for the enrichment of the plankton. Immense shoals of small anchovies gorge on the plankton, and their numbers, estimated at 10 million million are, in their turn, preyed upon by bonito and other fish, by sea lions and even by sperm whales, and by millions of sea birds such as albatrosses, shearwaters, petrels, gulls and terns, and especially by cormorants, pelicans and boobies (the southern gannets). Frank M. Chapman has described how the countless numbers of birds fishing the Current passed in endless undulating lines from one fishing ground to another, their sinuous files "crawling" through the air in repeated curves lost in the distance, with rarely a break in their ranks during the entire day. They traveled in solid "rivers" when feeding at distant grounds, and a single formation took four or five hours to pass a given point. Others were massed in great rafts on the sea, the cormorants floating in dense black packs, waiting for the processes of digestion to afford space for still more anchovies. Flocks of hundreds of boobies disappeared instantaneously from the sky when, as one bird, they plunged impetuously seaward in endless cataracts from a height of 50 feet and vanished in jets of spurting spray as they hit the surface.

There are estimated to be between three and five million cormorants on Peru's Islas de Chincha alone, and in one year the average catch of anchovies by birds and fishermen in this belt of the Humboldt Current, 800 miles long by 30 miles wide, amounted to more than 10 million tons—about one-fifth of the world's total haul of fish.

The barrier of the thermocline is broken not only by strong

currents but also by the presence of submarine banks near the surface, which disturb the seas. And wherever two currents meet in the ocean there is turbulence, in which the surface waters sink and the deep waters bearing nutrient salts rise to regenerate the plankton. To observe the effect of this phenomenon on all kinds of marine organisms is the most illuminating introduction one can have to life in the ocean. Robert Cushman Murphy has recorded a graphic description of current turbulence at night off the coast of Colombia. On either side, and at a bafflingly uncertain distance from his ship, the *Askoy*, a dark line like a wall of advancing water appeared to be closing in, and he could hear the splash and murmur of a troubled surface. Then there was a gleam of foam sprinkled with points of luminescence on the slowly approaching swell, which proved, however, to be no more than dancing water, tossing little peaks a mere foot or so into the air and beating a tattoo on the steel flanks of the *Askoy*. But soon a sharp hissing sound, different from the hissing of small waves, came out of the darkness to starboard and was followed by the strange sighings and puffings of blackfish (pilot whales) rolling and lumbering along and eventually diving to pass beneath the ship, with a bacchanalian clamor of rumblings and belchings. The long beam of the ship's searchlight revealed that the hissing was caused by the leapings of small fish, which could be seen shooting into the air and pouring down like hail for as far as the light carried; and that the surface of the sea was seething and boiling with life—larvae of clawless lobsters, tinted jellyfish, chains of the transparent, barrel-shaped, jelly-like salps, small herring-like fish, a silvery hatchet fish with its face bitten off, rudder fish hanging head downward, luminous lantern fish with shining red and purple lights, and swimming crabs. A to this upwelling of the sea's harvest were birds—boobies, stormy petrels, tropic and frigate birds, and even a flock of northern phalaropes from the far north, which were picking out small game from crevices in the logs stranded among the jetsam. But there were also great turtles drifting along, as motionless and barnacled as the logs above them; sea snakes undulating past with golden-spotted tails flashing when they turned to look up at the ship; sharks rising from far down in the deeps; and schools of tens of thousands of young yellow-tailed amberjacks being hunted by a herd of five or six hundred dolphins. Squids, from villainous blood-red atoms 2 inches long to 8-foot monsters, rocketed with ferocious speed at snowy-winged immature flying fish; and wine-colored pelagic crabs with purple swimming legs, many-toothed claws, and eyes wavering on long stalks, scavenged on fragments chopped up by the squids; while halfbeak fish shot through the turbulence as swiftly as the squids, scooping up plankton with their protruding, toothless lower jaws. From what distances had all these predators traveled to feast on this thin line of riches, and in what way were they informed of its existence?

At one point in her beautiful interpretation of life in the ocean, Rachel Carson wrote, with some poetic license, "Fishes and plankton, whales and squid, birds and sea-turtles, all are linked with unbreakable ties to certain kinds of water—to warm or cold water, clear or turbid water, to water rich in phosphates or silicates. . . . Temperature is probably the most important single condition that controls the distribution of marine animals." This is an overstatement. There are great navigators in the ocean. Salmon travel 2,000 or 3,000 miles through Pacific and Atlantic waters to their spawning rivers, gray whales migrate 6,000 miles from their winter breeding grounds off Baja California to their summer fishing waters in the Bering Sea, and blue whales travel halfway around the globe on their mysterious migrations. These and others like them must traverse warm and cold seas, rich and barren seas. And if all forms of marine life are restricted to waters with a limited range of temperature, how can young angler fish and other deep-water fry that have hatched in surface waters with a temperature of between 68 and 77 degrees F descend in a sudden and rapid migration to adult depths where the temperature is almost constantly between 35 and 40 degrees F? Furthermore, how can those fish and squids and crustaceans whose daytime levels are below 1,000 feet rise safely near sunset to feed in surface waters? Those living at such depths in equatorial waters of the Atlantic will have to adapt themselves to a swift change from a temperature of about 50 degrees F to one of 70 degrees F, and will experience in one night a climacteric that residents in upper waters will experience only in the course of a year.

This is not to imply that water temperatures are not of vital importance to most marine life. They particularly affect spawning fish. Adult cod, for example, can survive in seas whose temperature is only a degree or two above freezing point, but they cannot spawn in waters below 35 or 40 degrees F. By contrast, swordfish migrate in the summer to seas with temperatures in the low fifties, but must spawn in tropical waters where temperatures are not lower than 70 degrees F. It is also true that sudden fluctuations in temperature, rare on a wide scale in the ocean, can have catastrophic effects. During a gale in the spring of 1882, ships in the Atlantic reported millions of dead and dying tilefish floating over an area of from 5,000 to 7,000 square miles off the northeast United States. These had apparently succumbed to the effects of cold water from the Arctic flooding into their zone of distribution after northerly gales. Millions of dead capelins, fish of the smelt family, are also reported from time to time in the Barents Sea, where very sudden rises in temperature occur—for a rise in temperature can be as deadly as a fall. It might also be argued that temperature may limit the range of such flightless sea birds as penguins, whose most northerly outposts are to be found on coasts washed by the cold Humboldt and Benguela Currents, and coincide with the 68-degree F isotherm, which is influenced by ocean currents. It could be assumed that penguins cannot tolerate higher temperatures than this and that, as they evolved in the Southern Hemisphere, they cannot now pass north through the barrier presented by the warm equatorial waters.

Perhaps what Rachel Carson had specifically in mind, when referring to the importance of temperature, were disasters similar to those attributed to the periodic southerly extension of the current known as El Niño, which has been cited again and again as the basic cause of the "crash" in the populations of fish and birds off the coast of Peru that occurs every seven years or so and is of catastrophic proportions at intervals of about thirty years. According to tradition, El Niño, a warm current, tends to flow farther south than normal about every seventh year. At very much longer intervals, when abnormally weak air circulations are prevalent, it is able to sweep more than 1,000 miles farther south, to the vicinity of Lima, before fusing with the cold Humboldt Current; while at the same time, instead of being blown offshore by the southeast trade winds, El Niño's warm tropical waters are wedged between the coast and the Humboldt Current. In these conditions, the barrier presented by the tropically warm surface waters prohibits the upwelling of the nutrient-rich cold waters of the Humboldt Current; plankton and billions of anchovies die, and the sea is polluted by the myriads of dead organisms and the proliferating bacteria. Millions of breeding cormorants, pelicans and boobies, together with their young, starve. The supplies of commercially valuable guano on the nesting rocks are not replenished, Peru's national income is drastically reduced, and her wretched poor become poorer—if that is possible.

Certainly all these disasters occur at more or less regular intervals, but they may not necessarily be due to a southerly extension of El Niño. It is equally possible that the cessation of the prevailing southeast trade winds permits excessive heating of the sea by solar radiation down to exceptional depths, and that this prevents the upwelling of the cold waters beneath. In these conditions the temperature of the Humboldt Current may rise by 10 degrees in forty-eight hours and it suffers a sea change, "here reddened by acres of living jelly, there streaked with a Milky Way of swimming crablets perhaps no less numerous than the stars," as Robert Cushman Murphy described it. "Leaping mantas, schools of large flying-fish pursued by equally alien tropical dolphin-fish, and thousands upon thousands of immigrant hammer-head sharks crossed our course. Their line of march was perhaps two miles broad and of indefinite length, for we cut through it at widely separated points." Without an upwelling of nutrient salts, there is no food for the diatoms on which the anchovies feed, and the chain of disaster will have begun—a disaster which the Peruvians are now actively assisting by overfishing: when 9 million tons of anchovies were landed in 1965, a reported 20 million sea birds perished.

If disasters on the El Niño scale were a common and widespread phenomenon in the ocean, nature would indeed be hard-pressed to maintain the balance of her marine economy, and we know that she does have problems in controlling the astronomical multitudes of planktonic life. A spell of calm weather over warm seas may result in the imperfectly understood phenomenon of red water, known to the Peruvians as the Callao Painter. These red tides are colored by inconceivable numbers of the plankton *Gymnodinium brevis*, a dinoflagellate, in densities variously estimated at from 5 to 60 million per quart of water. Large numbers of marine animals are poisoned by the toxins from this plankton. A reported 50 million fish died off Florida in 1946 and 1947 from the combined effects of poisoning and lack of oxygen, since the latter is absorbed by the bacteria multiplying on the dead fish and on the dinoflagellates themselves when their multimillions have exhausted the supplies of nutrients.

But dinoflagellate conflagrations are not restricted to warm seas. Autumnal seas off the Pacific coast of North America may become polluted by another dinoflagellate, *Gonyaulax*, which also secretes a virulent poison. A few days after *Gonyaulax*'s "blooming," fish and shellfish are affected, and the toxins accumulated in the livers of mussels react on the human nervous system like strychnine. As recently as May 1968 a relatively small concentration of another toxic dinoflagellate occurred in the North Sea off the coast of Northumberland, England. This resulted in the deaths of vast numbers of sand eels, and of more than three-quarters of the shags nesting on the Farne Islands and a lesser number of the islands' terns, which had been feasting on the sand eels. Seventy-eight cases of shellfish poisoning among humans who had eaten toxic mussels were also reported. In subsequent years this pollution has occurred in a milder form, virtually localities, where the waters of the sea's upper and lower levels never mix, and where the deeps are never reoxygenated by sinking cold water, the concentrations of hydrogen sulphide may be permanently excessive. Such conditions prevail in the Bay of Naples, in some of the Norwegian fiords and, notably, in the Black Sea, where the depths between 600 and 6,000 feet are virtually lifeless.

It is in maintaining the ocean's population equilibrium that nature must experience her most perplexing problems. Certain shrimps, for example, feed extensively on the young of the krill, which, being among the giants of the zooplankton (jellyfish excepted), require two years or more to mature into handsome crustaceans with green thoraxes filled with chlorophyll-impregnated diatoms, and heads and abdomens stained orange with the latter's carotene. Normally supply and demand are in balance; but there are years when the shrimps multiply excessively and deplete the numbers of krill so critically that herds of whales face starvation when they return to Antarctic waters the following summer. No computer could cope with the ocean's logistic problems. One ingenious biologist has estimated that a single herring may have in its stomach six or seven thousand copepods—crustaceans, ranging in size from those no bigger than a pin's head to *Calanus*, which is as large as a grain of rice. Yet each of these copepods contains 130,000 diatoms. But if a medium-sized whale, such as a 45-foot humpback, must consume a ton of herrings or five thousand individual fish to sustain it for a few hours, then 400 trillion diatoms have been expended in satisfying the requirements of this simple food-chain.

It is true that there are only a few tens of thousands of whales directly dependent upon plankton for food, and they can have little effect on the ocean's stocks of plankton in normal circumstances. But consider the quantities of plankton required to support the tens of millions of sea birds, the infinitely greater number of herrings and other fish, and the still more astronomical numbers of small squids, whose luminous masses cover the surface waters of all the oceans at night for mile after mile, and whose assemblies of mating males and egg-laying females cover hundreds of acres of the sea floor. There is no need to stress further the catastrophic breakdown in the ocean's food-chains that would ensue, should the plankton harvest fail over a wide area.

One presumes that no such catastrophe has ever occurred and that nature has always been able to limit dinoflagellate conflagrations—although there were four off Florida in the 1950s—and to control excessive multiplication of predators. She may, however, be fighting a losing battle in the Pacific against the depredations of the crown-of-thorns, a large starfish whose disk may span 24 inches and whose fifteen to seventeen arms are spiked with hundreds of poisonous 2-inch spines. The crown-of-thorns eats living coral at the rate of 2 square feet a night, possibly by killing the polyps with a toxin. During the past decade its numbers have multiplied to such a degree that it is in the process of eating up not only the coral reefs of various Pacific islands but also those of the Great Barrier Reef off Australia. Estimates of the extent and destructiveness of its depredations are confused and contradictory, but nine-tenths of the coral along 38 miles of Guam's shoreline and one-quarter of the 1,200-mile-long Barrier Reef are reported to have been destroyed. If the crown-of-thorns is in fact destroying not only the veneer of living coral but also the basic structure of the reefs, then as the dead coral disintegrates, so the lagoons within the reefs will be exposed to the sea's swell and their fish and other inhabitants will lose their special environment. In wondering why nature has suddenly lost control over the activities of these monstrous starfish, we note that they are numerous wherever there is human settlement. Has man therefore been responsible for their population explosion—perhaps by the simple act of overcollecting the giant 14-inch triton mollusks that prey on them, or by killing with some pollutant discharged into the sea the zooplankton that prey on the crown-of-thorns' larvae? It is possibly significant that this area of the Pacific has been exposed to contamination by nuclear radiation. It will be interesting to see if nature can regain control over the crown-of-thorns before all the coral reefs in the Pacific have been affected.

2: Feeding Habits of the
Great Whales and Sharks

It is remarkable that the largest known animal, the blue whale, which averages 80 feet in length and 120 tons in weight, should feed exclusively on plankton; but plankton is present in such quantities and is so nutritious and rich in vitamins A and D that all the larger whales except the sperm whale feed partly or wholly on such food, whether it be the relatively large shrimplike krill, the pteropods (the swimming snails), which are rarely more than a quarter of an inch long, or the minute crustacean copepods. The two largest sharks—the basking shark, reaching a length of 40 feet or more, and the monstrous whale shark, reaching 60 and possibly 70 feet —also feed on plankton. So do other giant fish, such as the 8- or 10-foot sunfish, which is almost as broad as it is long and more than a ton in weight, and the 3,000-pound manta ray, whose pectoral fins have developed into bat-wings 22 feet across.

In order to capture sufficient quantities of food to nourish their immense bulk, the exclusively plankton-feeding whales, such as the blue whale and the bowhead, must necessarily possess very large mouths. The enormous mouth, 20 feet long and 12 feet wide, of the bowhead is proportionately very much longer than that of a blue whale, amounting to a third of its overall length. But the relatively small mouth size of the blue whale and other rorquals such as the finback may perhaps be offset by the curious pleats that form 2-inch deep grooves in their throats. A blue whale possesses about sixty of these, and a finback whale about a hundred. The function of these pleats has not been definitely established, but it has been plausibly suggested that they enable a rorqual's throat to be greatly expanded when it is feeding with mouth open and tongue depressed. That this may be their function is perhaps confirmed by the fact that the sperm whale, which swallows the largest squids whole, also possesses more than thirty pleats.

Each kind of plankton-feeder has its own special mechanism for capturing its food. When a basking shark is feeding, it cruises open-mouthed just below the surface at 2 knots, siphoning in through its 3-foot wide gape twenty or thirty tons of water a minute and, with the water, the teeming *Calanus* copepods—the rice-grain-sized crustacean—and euphausiids—the small shrimplike crustacean. The inner sides of the five immense gill-clefts encircling its neck are furnished with rakers resembling the teeth of a comb, thirty-two to the inch. When the gills open wide, a band of muscle erects the two rows of rakers, and they interlock to form a sieve that filters the plankton from the water passing out over the gills. Hence the shark's slow cruising speed gives him efficient filtering.

The manta ray, swinging along near the surface with

regular upward and downward beats of its "wings," like a monstrous brown bird, employs a somewhat similar feeding technique. By stretching sideways and then flapping together the grotesque earlike lobes that project from its head like horns, it sweeps tons of small crustaceans and other plankton into the cavern of its mouth and up against a fine lattice-work in the throat. The latter acts as a gill-strainer and also retains the plankton until they can be swallowed in conveniently small masses.

Just as the two great sharks, the ray and, for that matter, small fish such as herrings employ gill-rakers as plankton retainers, and crab-eater seals are equipped with deeply serrated teeth that lock to form a sieve, so the plankton-feeding whales have evolved horny baleen ("whalebone") plates less than ⅓ inch thick, and thinner still in the case of the sei whales, which feed mainly on *Calanus*, the small copepods. These plates, which, like the human fingernail, are composed of keratin, hang down in fringes from the roof of the mouth. The bowhead possesses 350 or more, each 10 to 15 feet long, whereas those of the blue whale, with its proportionately smaller mouth, are a mere 3½ feet in length. As the whale cruises, open-mouthed, the vast mass of water sucked in swirls around the lower jaw, and the krill or copepods are entangled in the dense mat of baleen. The whale then closes its mouth and presses its huge tongue upward, jamming the krill against the mat of baleen, while allowing the water to pour along the outside of its jaws to a notch at the hind angle of its lips, from which it jets out into the sea. The tongue then scoops back the krill and passes them into the gullet.

With plankton available throughout the year in one area or another of the tropical seas which are their home, whale sharks and manta rays have no food problems. The former, indeed, probably feed as much, or more, on such small fish as sardines and anchovies, and also on small squids, as on plankton. For although a whale shark's gill-clefts are filled with a spongy filtering mechanism, whose texture is fine enough to retain all organisms exceeding $\frac{1}{8}$ inch, its enormous mouth (5 or 6 feet wide and cavernous enough when agape to contain two crouching men) is equipped with several thousand minute recurved teeth. Since these denticles are set in immense sheets around the jaws, their function is not to bite or crunch but to prevent the escape of free-swimming prey. In this respect Stewart Springer has described a rare encounter with a large number of schools of blackfin tuna, probably averaging 4 to 6 pounds, in smooth waters in the Gulf of Mexico. The tuna were apparently feeding on shoals of small fish less than 3 inches long and in the center of almost every shoal of tuna, at intervals of about a quarter of a mile, for as far as he could see, was a whale shark. "Pumping" vertically up and down in a 15-to-20 second cycle the whale shark's head would now be flush with the surface and then about 30 inches out of the sea. And as it sank down, the water would pour into its open mouth, no doubt carrying with it drafts of the small fish on which the tuna were feeding. As its mouth filled with water, so the shark would rise again, with the water streaming out of its gill-slits, to repeat the cycle. Although Springer was unable to confirm that the sharks were actually feeding on the small fish, because the tuna were continually striking at the cascades of water about the sharks' mouths and churning up the sea all around, he did see several tuna leap into the nearest shark's mouth whenever its head sank down, and he believed that it swallowed a considerable number of them.

UNIVERSITY OF WINNIPEG
LIBRARY
515 Portage Avenue
Winnipeg, Manitoba R3B 2E9

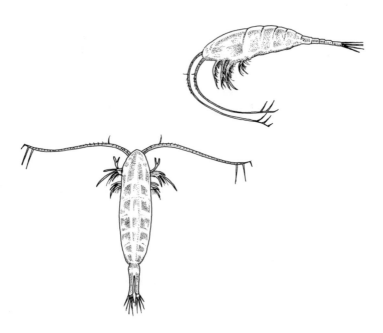

Copepod Calanus

indeed no perennially resident populations of oceanic fish in the surface waters of northern seas.

In the late autumn the majority of the baskers disappear once more from these North Atlantic coastal seas and are not seen in numbers again until the following spring. What happens to them? We are in possession of only two hard facts about their history during their mysterious six-month absence. The first is that solitary baskers are sighted fairly frequently during this interim period, the second is that stranded specimens, and therefore presumably all the others too, shed their gill-rakers during the winter months. From these two facts it follows that, even if there were sufficient plankton, the sharks could not secure food, and the presence of solitary individuals suggests that there may not be any general emigration. Since no one has ever recorded seeing schools of them "basking" in surface waters during the winter, Harrison Matthews, who has studied them both at sea and in the laboratory more extensively than most zoologists, has suggested that in order to avoid excessive loss of energy and fat reserves during these months of enforced starvation, they may rest tranquilly near the sea bottom, perhaps in deep canyons off the edge of the continental shelf, in what might be described as a state of suspended animation. This hypothesis must be qualified by the fact that in Californian waters baskers are present throughout the year. During this presumed period of tranquillity the females of the Atlantic baskers will be in the final stages of pregnancy, for the young sharks are apparently born in the spring, about the time that the schools, equipped with newly grown gill-rakers, move into coastal waters.

Whale (Balaena Biscayensis)

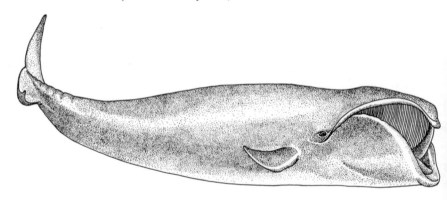

This short résumé of what we do not know about basking sharks emphasizes the extraordinary problems confronting marine biologists who try to observe their subject in the elusive waters of the ocean, for in 1972 we still know no more about the basking shark's life history than we did after Matthews had concluded his research in Hebridean seas more than twenty years ago. There is room and to spare in the unknown ocean for tens of thousands of sharp-eyed and experienced biologists.

A somewhat similar problem is presented by the plankton-feeding whales. When plankton is out of season, the lesser rorqual (also known as red or piked) whales and the northern races of humpback and fin whales can feed on cuttlefish, mackerel, capelin, whiting and especially herring. But how do those that are exclusively dependent on plankton survive? Since their appetites are so immense, they are necessarily predominantly inhabitants of cold seas, where the densest concentrations of krill and copepods are located. The bow-

Skeleton of the whale (Balaena Biscayensis)

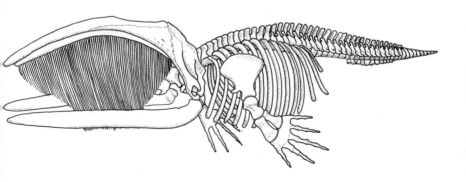

heads are, for example, resident in the Arctic—or were, until those in the North Atlantic were virtually exterminated by whalers. They never migrated out of Arctic waters, merely moving with the ice-front as polar seas froze over, but there is no evidence as to how they survived during the winter months.

So too, in the Antarctic, the extension of the ice-pack in May and June cuts off most of the supplies of krill. In this instance, however, the majority of the southern populations of blue whales, fin whales and humpbacks emigrate and set off on their largely unknown voyages, though a few individuals are apparently permanently resident in Antarctic seas. Some of their migrations may be almost global in extent, for, some blue whales are known to travel halfway around the world, from 60°E to 125°W. While both the fin whales and humpbacks winter in South African and South American seas, the latter also visit the Indian Ocean off Madagascar and Australian and New Zealand waters. Even the warm seas of the tropical Atlantic doldrums are visited by herds of rorquals. But though their widely scattered herds may winter in these subtropical and sub-Antarctic seas which contain plankton, and though, unlike the basking sharks, they are apparently continually on the move, they do not in fact migrate primarily in search of fresh feeding grounds. Of two thousand humpbacks harpooned off an eastern Australian whaling station only one had food in its stomach. And blue whales are thin when they return to the Antarctic in the early summer of October or November. However, since by any reasonable estimate a large whale's daily food requirements must be measured in tons, it is difficult to credit that it could survive four to six months' total starvation, as has been suggested, despite the immense reserve of food it carries in the layer of blubber which covers the greater part of its body in thicknesses varying from about 4 inches in the case of a small fin whale to 11 or 12 inches in that of a blue whale. Only on the flippers, fins and tail flukes is the blubber reduced to an essential minimum for efficiency in swimming. Loss of heat in these thinly covered extremities is apparently prevented by an ingenious arrangement whereby the arteries carrying warm blood are closely surrounded by veins bringing back cooled blood. Thus the blood flowing outwards warms the blood returning from the chilled extremities.

During this period of partial or total starvation the calves are born, and a blue whale has to supply her calf with a ton of very rich milk every twenty-four hours. Since the calf cannot remain submerged for longer than half a minute, the cow suckles it while lying close beneath the surface, pumping gallons of milk at a time down its throat. This she is able to do because her mammary glands contain large reservoirs from which the milk can be forcibly ejected by muscular contraction into the teats, which when not in use lie retracted within slits on either side of her genital opening. As a result of this generous feeding the calf doubles its weight in its first seven days, and by the time it is weaned after six or seven months has added 30 feet to its birth length of between 22 and 25 feet; at the age of two years, when it is 75 feet and weighs 60 tons, it is itself sexually mature. There is no parallel among mammals to this plankton-stimulated growth rate of the blue whale.

Whether the baleen whales do or do not feed during their long absence from the Antarctic is therefore to some extent of academic interest, as there appears to be a more fundamental reason why they must emigrate—namely, to ensure that the calves will be born during their sojourn in warmer seas, though even the approximate localities of their breeding areas in these seas are still not known. No doubt the adults are insulated by their thick layer of blubber against loss of body heat in polar seas, though it is true that sperm whales, ranging mainly through the tropics—for only the bulls migrate into the Antarctic—may be even more heavily blubbered. It is reasonable to assume that the newborn and young nursing calves, covered with only a thin layer of blubber, would lose body heat so rapidly in cold seas that they could not survive if born in the Antarctic, though it has been claimed that theoretically their blubber layer is thick enough to retain adequate heat in the coldest waters. However that may be, by the time the herds return to the Antarctic the calves' blubber has thickened and their baleen plates have developed into efficient plankton-collectors.

The enormous quantity of plankton essential to sustain a large whale, which may have 2 tons of krill in its stomach at one time, is emphasized by the probability that only about a thousandth part of that consumed can be diverted into the energy required to thrust the whale's great bulk through the ocean. Whales are now known to be considerably heavier than was formerly believed, weighing about $1\frac{1}{2}$ tons per foot of length. The largest blue whale captured exceeded 113 feet in length and weighed 170 tons, while a 90-foot cow weighed 136 tons. Strings of figures of lengths and weights can convey little impression of the gigantic proportions of the great plankton-feeding whales. However, the liver of a blue whale weighs 1 ton and its heart almost half a ton, while it carries in its mouth almost the equivalent of a full-grown elephant in the form of a tongue that weighs 4 tons. "There is nothing that reduces man to his proper dimensions more rapidly and completely than contemplation of a fully grown blue whale at play in the open ocean," wrote Ivan

Sanderson, who when nine years old gave a practical demonstration of the blue whale's immensity by wriggling through the main artery of a 70-foot specimen.

Since their immense bulk is buoyed by water, whales can attain dimensions vastly greater than any land animal, and there is indeed no physical reason why there should not be larger creatures than blue whales in the ocean, providing that adequate supplies of food could be found for such monsters. When the linear dimensions of an animal are doubled, its volume—and therefore its weight—is increased eight times. If this doubling up continued, the skeleton of a land animal would collapse beneath its own weight. But in the sea, the greater an animal's mass, the more room there is for muscles that generate swimming power to overcome the frictional drag of water, which is eight hundred times denser than air. The rear one-third of a blue whale is an engine of enormous muscles, driving the 12-foot tail flukes up and down comparatively slowly, but displacing a large volume of water. Whether or not, as often stated, the flukes execute a semi-rotary sculling motion similar to that of a ship's two-bladed screw is, again, academic. The drive comes from the volume of water displaced, and it has been estimated that a 90-foot blue whale generates 500 horsepower, with its flukes exerting a drive twenty times more efficient than a ship's propellor of similar dimensions. In the main, whales are leisurely cruisers, with blue, fin and sperm whales averaging 10 or 12 knots, and humpbacks and bowheads no more than 4 knots. But a blue whale can maintain its distance all day from a whaler doing 10 knots, and can raise this speed to 20 knots when pressed. Ivan Sanderson describes how on three consecutive days a 60-foot fin whale cruised for hours on end only a few feet ahead of the bows of a Diesel-powered, twin-screwed yacht, with no more effort than a slight twitching of its flukes. Although the yacht was traveling at speeds of up to 20 knots, the fin whale would sometimes forge away from it at apparently twice that speed. There is a bona fide record of a school of dolphins playing around a U.S. destroyer doing 32 knots, and bottle-nosed dolphins have been timed to do 30 knots. Although such speeds are theoretically three times faster than is hydrodynamically possible, they are achieved partly by efficient streamlining and partly by what can be crudely described as a pliable skin that reduces drag by means of minute corrugations lubricated by natural body oils—whose efficiency is the despair of naval architects.

3: Life in the Deeps

When men speak of the ocean they are recalling its surface waters—the sunlit blue seas of the tropics, the ice-green Arctic waters, or the cold gray waves of queasy storm-tossed crossings. Whales pass many hours in herculean play on the surface of the ocean, rolling, cavorting and breaching. But this is not the world that fish and plankton inhabit. Beneath the surface are 330 million cubic miles almost unknown to man. Here is a world that could inspire greater literature, art and photography than man has yet produced; a world in which the fish swim through waters of a limpid pastel blue, or, in Gilbert Klingel's words, "A filmy evanescent blue that shimmers with the faint lustre of a pearl conceived by clarity and sunlight: the most exquisite hue I have ever seen. I felt drowned in it, as though I were floating in space with pure azure above, below and beneath."

Although the phytoplankton can draw energy from the sun when 300 feet below the surface, the red has already disappeared from the spectrum at one-third or one-fifth of that depth. The French pioneers of the Mediterranean's underwater world were horrified to see green blood flowing from the fish they had speared and their own green blood welling from cuts on their hands when they were only 60 feet down.

At the lower limit of the photosynthetic zone the yellow-greens are lost and the blue deepens with a terrible slowness, through a brilliant twilight of dark blue to a blacker blue with the faintest tinge of violet, and then to the most intense blackish-blue a man could conceive—as Beebe wrote. At 1,500 feet the last trace of blue has been filtered from the black, and at 3,000 feet the waters are blacker than any blackness imaginable in the earth world. The ultimate depth to which earth light penetrates the oceans depends upon the angle at which the sun's rays strike the surface and upon the clarity of the water in a particular locality. Since the eyes of fish are even more sensitive than those of man, which, after a period of adjustment to darkness, can detect light only one-ten-million-millionth the strength of full sunlight, it can be assumed that they can discern the last faint glimmer at depths between 2,500 feet and 3,000 feet.

Until quite recently it was generally believed that there was no life in the black abyss, and that even the midwaters, a few hundred feet below the surface, were only sparsely populated. But we now know that there are at least two thousand species of midwater, or bathypelagic, and bottom, or benthic, fish swimming happily about their business at depths below 750 feet, and one wonders how many more are still to be discovered. When Beebe dived 3,000 feet in his bathysphere in Bermudan waters he found the deep fauna of the Sargasso Sea to be rich beyond all his expectations, which were based on the numerous deep trawls he had made previously in this "desert" of the ocean. But despite his findings, the myth of the Sargasso as a desert persisted into the 1960s, when the biologists of a research vessel expressed surprise at the richness of the midwater fauna. It should now have been established once and for all that in the 750-to-4,500-foot zone the Sargasso is in fact richer in plankton and fish than are the seas beyond. One would have thought this could naturally be assumed, since its depths are being continually fertilized and replenished with food from the decomposing weed and dead animals sinking from the 6,000 square miles of sargassum weed scattered over the surface above. However, the bathypelagic, or midwater, fish are essentially the inhabitants of tropical and subtropical seas. No deep-living fish are known to be resident in the Arctic, for example, though some thirty kinds of lantern fish are to be found in the midwaters of the Antarctic.

We now have a truer, though still very incomplete understanding of the distribution of life in the ocean deeps. Broadly speaking, the upper 300 feet, especially the 30 feet of surface water, are the plankton's world, though at night this level is visited by countless millions of predatory fish and crustaceans from deeper waters. In the 1,500-to-3,500-foot zone the concentration of zooplankton is normally only one-tenth of that in the surface levels, and it continues to diminish downward. Since plant life capable of photosynthesis virtually ceases at a depth of 300 feet, it has been generally assumed that the only plant-eating animals in the midwaters must be those that ascend, toward earth night, into the phytoplankton levels, and that the majority of the other inhabitants of the abyss must be carnivorous upon each other or, if bottom-living, must scavenge on detritus. But this assumption ignores the fact that other forms of plant life, the coccolithophores, a minute flagellate, flourish in concentrations of ¼ million to 1 quart of water at depths of 12,000 feet or deeper, subsisting on dissolved organic matter and the excreta of zooplankton. Although these dwarf plankton are so minute that the largest, at 1/1000th of an inch, can be captured only with the finest cheesecloth nets, and the remainder only by separation from the water with a centrifuge, their total mass may equal or possibly exceed that of diatoms and dinoflagellates combined, for at higher levels their numbers are twenty times greater and are responsible for the phenomenon of "white water," which fishermen associate with shoals of herring. It is the presence of this mass of microscopic plankton, rather than of some still-undiscovered food source, that presumably accounts for reports from a number of widely separated localities of marked increases in the concentrations of zooplankton in the 2,500-to-3,500-foot levels, and perhaps at greater depths. We do not know how deep the zooplankton can exist. Georges Houot and Pierre Willm noted souplike masses of planktonic life throughout the course of their 13,000-foot bathysphere dive 160 miles off the coast of northwest Africa. Jacques Piccard, on the other hand, did not observe a trace of plankton in the Mariana Trench in the southwest Pacific, where the majority of the trenches are located. There, in the Challenger Deep, the water was crystal clear in the cone of his bathyscaphe's searchlight—"a vast emptiness beyond all comprehension."

There is yet another source of food in the abyss—the ultramicroscopic bacteria. There are too many hungry animals in the ocean for any corpse to sink more than a few fathoms before being carved up, picked clean or swallowed whole—

unless it is dissolved under pressure. But for millennium after millennium a ceaseless "snowstorm" of dead algae and plankton has continued sinking, sinking, sinking through the depths—Rimbaud's "green nights of extravagant snow"—blanketing the ocean bottom with deposits thousands of feet thick of pteropods (a gastropod mollusk), of diatom ooze and of radiolarian ooze composed of silica. There lie millions of square miles of *Globigerina* (a small rhizopod) shells and still more millions, in the ultimate depths, of volcanic red clay, in which nothing is found except those permanent insolubles resistant to the greatest pressures—sharks' teeth and the otoliths, or ear stones, of whales. There can be little doubt that on the bottom, and probably in the midwaters too, there exist forms of bacteria as numerous as those in the earth's soil. These subsist, uniquely, on the inorganic compounds of such minerals as nitrates and sulphur, and convert the cellulose and chitin of shells and skeletons into substances upon which crustacea and other invertebrates can feed. These in turn provide food for deep and bottom fish. The earliest primitive colonizers of the ocean floor must have found there some source of food, and if this was not bacteria, what was it?

From the sunlit surface world, down through the twilight levels to darkness or near darkness at a depth of 2,500 feet, is the main zone of fish and squids. During the next 2,500 feet their numbers thin out, though they are still sparsely distributed down to 20,000 feet. During a two-year voyage of 60,000 miles, the Danish research ship *Galathea* dredged up 140 species of animals from depths below 18,000 feet. And as deep as man has descended into the abyss, a depth of almost 36,000 feet in the Challenger Deep, he has found life.

A thousand feet below the Red Sea, Cousteau saw transparent fish whose red and black internal organs were visible within their glassy bodies, and other unknown fish with protuberant jaws digging holes under boulders with their tails. There were tricolor shrimps with spectacularly long antennae and hosts of small squids standing on their heads while whirling like dervishes and, at the same time, turning their mantles and arms inside out—possibly in some frenzied escape reaction.

Beebe describes how, when his bathysphere was at a depth of more than 2,000 feet during his half-mile dive into the Sargasso, two fish with very large eyes swam slowly past the porthole at a distance of not more than 6 or 8 feet. They were at least 6 feet long and resembled large barracudas, though with shorter undershot jaws armed with numerous fangs. The latter were illumined either by mucus or by indirect internal lights, while single lines of strong pale bluish lights were strung along their bodies, and two long tentacles depended from their chins and from the region of their tails. Each of the tentacles was tipped with a pair of separate twitching and jerking luminous bodies, of which the upper was reddish, the lower blue. By their vertical fins, placed well back, Beebe recognized them as members of the family of sea dragons and named them *Bathysphaera intacta*, the "untouchable fish."

Large fish have been encountered at much greater depths than 2,000 feet. There are sharks up to 10 feet long, with shovel-shaped snouts to their broad flat heads, at 4,200 feet in the Mediterranean. Small Portuguese sharks have been caught in traps at depths of almost 9,000 feet. When Georges Houot and Pierre Willm's bathysphere was resting in a garden of anemones on the 13,000-foot bottom off Dakar it

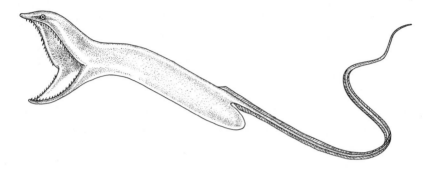

Gulper eel

was visited by 6- or 7-foot sharks, characteristically inquisitive. Nevertheless the extraordinary and grotesque predatory
adaptations exhibited by the fish of the abyss indicate that
food in the form of other fish, squids, shrimps or prawns
must be at least relatively scarce. And Beebe noted that
despite their clumsy-looking globular and angular shapes
they were as active as the predators of upper waters. Many
are little more than animate eating-machines whose every
function is subordinated to the capture and digestion of
infrequent prey, and whose rows of appalling saber-like
teeth of uneven length are too large to be confined within
their mouths. Gigantic and cavernous mouths reach what
must surely be their final evolution in one species of gulper,
well named the pelican eel, whose body virtually consists of
only a gaping mouth of folded skin, capable of engulfing the
rare prey lured by the lantern light on its head. Since its
jaws are several times the length of its skull, it can, when
opening its mouth—one would hardly exaggerate in sub-
stituting "chest" for "mouth"—force its backbone back upon

itself in a sharp fold, while engorging its prey with a snake-like action of jaws working independently and alternately. Distensible stomachs enable other abyssal fish to engorge prey three times their own length, transforming them in the process into pendulous balloons. Were the majority not diminutive, less than 6 inches long (assuming that specimens captured in deep trawls are typical), they would be creatures of the most horrendous nightmare ever to shame Franken-stein and his monster. They have indeed been described as suffering from congenital rickets because of the absence of ultraviolet rays and the imbalance of phosphorus and cal-cium in the abyss. But grotesque as they may appear to the human eye, we cannot escape the truth that they are in fact the inhabitants of more than three-fifths of this planet, since their world is that proportion of the earth that is covered with water more than a mile deep.

As in the deep waters, so on the ocean bottom man has found unsuspected activity. Many of the thousands of photo-graphs taken from Cousteau's ship *Calypso* at depths of between 2,500 and 16,000 feet in the Atlantic and Indian Oceans revealed that their bottoms are riddled with craters, cones and serpentine burrows. When the *Calypso* was towing a camera mounted on a sled over the bottom of the Mediter-ranean at depths of between 2,000 and 4,000 feet, it photo-graphed freshly excavated craters from 3 to 6 feet in diameter and up to 4 feet deep, which Cousteau surmised might have been made by hibernating basking sharks—though that does not seem very likely. His researches suggest that much of the bottom of the Mediterranean may be perforated with the holes of worms and other burrowers, and blistered with mounds up to 2 feet high. That the burrows in these mounds are inhabited is indicated by the activities of those heavy-

headed fish whose bodies taper to long, thin tails, the grenadiers or rattails. These can be seen exploring the mounds
with the sensory barbels beneath their chins, while grubbing
about with their heavily armored snouts, just as, in the continental shallows far above, goatfish, or surmullets, which
feed mainly at night on crustaceans, locate these with long
tactile chin barbels serving the dual purpose of mine-detectors
and taste organs. When not in use the barbels are retracted
into a groove beneath the surmullet's throat. But in order
to locate food in the total darkness of the ocean bottom, still
more sophisticated equipment is required; hence the development of disproportionately long threadlike tails and extraordinarily, bizarre extensions of the pelvic fins into sensory
feelers one and a half times as long as the body, with which
to explore the ooze.

The grenadiers, though relatives of the cod of the upper
waters, apparently inhabit the bottoms, and also the midwaters, of many oceans and must be among the most
numerous fish in the sea. Piccard observed them at a depth

Rattail fish

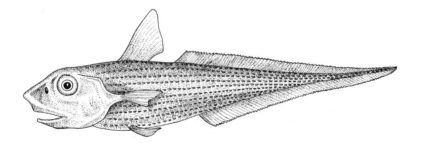

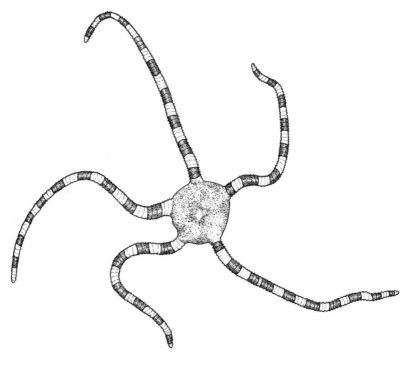

Brittle Star

of 4,200 feet on the bottom of the San Diego Trough off northwest Mexico, together with blind hagfish and the huge-eyed sablefish, known to the local fishermen as "black cod." This Trough, too, presented the appearance of having been plowed and churned by animal activity, and swarmed with brittle stars flailing their five long, snaking arms while feeding on detritus or walking with arched disk-shaped bodies over the ooze. Brittle stars must be the most plentiful of the ocean's benthic, or bottom, fauna, for there are photographs of their reptilian arms intertwining in dense tangles so thick that they cover the bottom. Photographs taken by the *Calypso*'s pinger-camera at a depth of more than 24,000 feet in the Romanche Trench off the Ivory Coast showed what were possibly brittle stars and also tiny fish shapes. Although the ocean bottom may not be universally soft, locomotion no doubt presents a problem; this has been solved by certain Japanese spider crabs with legs that span 15 feet.

There are bivalve mollusks in the Mindanao Trench off the Philippines and, surprisingly at such a depth, sunken rotting vegetation. Brotulid fish closely resembling the grenadiers are found in the Sunda Trench off Java, and an unknown species of fish, 12 inches long, at a depth of over 27,000 feet on the flat bottom of the Puerto Rico Trench. When Piccard reached the smooth ivory-colored floor of the Challenger Deep, the ocean's *ultima thule*, a red shrimp awaited his bathyscaphe and, to his amazement, a type of flatfish about 12 inches long and 6 inches across, with two round eyes on the top of its head. This was a true fish, resembling a sole—a vertebrate like man—enduring a pressure of 8 tons on every square inch of its body. "Slowly, extremely slowly, this flatfish swam away. Moving along the bottom, partly in the ooze and partly in the water, it disappeared into the night."

And what of the underwater world during the earth's night? It is now almost thirty years since Gilbert Klingel wrote of his diving experiences after being wrecked on Great Inagua, one of the Bahamas. Though he was hampered by the 80-pound helmet in which men dived in those early days, no diver since his time has given us such a beautiful conception of the submarine world. It was at 9:30 on a May evening that he dived in the inky water over an Inaguan reef to within 10 feet of the bottom:

Try as I might I could discern nothing. I was poised in the centre of empty space. There was neither light nor movement, only a still solid blackness. . . . I twisted around and saw nothing except the same utter void. . . . Revolving to my original position I saw a very wonderful event. Out of the darkness that covered the deep there suddenly blossomed into being a tiny pinpoint of light. It flared for perhaps a sixteenth of a second, reached a brilliance made all the more vivid by the dark all around and was extinguished. . . .

Then, as my eyes adjusted themselves to the dark, I began to see other flashes, minute explosions that burst suddenly into being and then passed for ever out of sight. Reaching for the searchlight I . . . pressed the button. Instantly a long beam of strong white light pierced the gloom and went pencilling off into the distance. I looked in vain for the makers of the tiny flashing lights, but they were nowhere to be seen. . . . Turning the beam off, I waited. . . . Sure enough the lights became visible once again, only this time I saw many more . . . a galaxy of little star-points, a cosmos of pale Fourth of July sparklers without the glowing stems. The lights were the energy-burstings of hundreds of microscopic animalcules, whose bodies, too small to be visible under natural illumination, were betrayed by the energy they expended.

Turning on the flash again I swept it in a wide arc. The lovely evanescent blue of daytime was gone; in its place was a long beam of yellow surrounded on each side by purplish gloom. The water, however, was crystal-clear, and the rays brilliantly brought into vision any objects within their reach. . . .

A brilliant flash many times brighter than the rays of the electric bulb suddenly burst back at me. It lasted for only a second and then vanished . . . in the space of an eyewink it was followed by another and another until the water was blazing with them. . . . These were no microscopic explosions but large blazes of coloured fire.

The flashes came closer, shooting across the beam with lightning rapidity, flaring and disappearing, approaching ever nearer. Finally one stopped only a few inches away. It was glowing from one end to the other with unearthly light, the most brilliant undiluted lavender I have ever seen. I recognized this lovely creature as an anchovy, a fish about three or four inches in length. . . . No opal ever gleamed with more intense fire; even as the anchovy moved the lavender was replaced with a shimmering pink and finally with a bright silver as it sped away.

The coming of the anchovies is an event that I shall long remember. There must have been some magnetic quality about my searchlight that they could not resist. . . . In less time than it takes to write this sentence, I was surrounded by a deluge of silver-lavender forms that milled about the lens in a whirling cloud, rushing headlong at the glass, bumping it and turning in sudden fright to dash away, only to be magnetized once more. The accumulated reflection of their shining bodies lit up the darkness for several yards around; ripples of rose-coloured light flickered through the murk.

Within five minutes there must have been several hundred of them, but these were completely eclipsed when from the surface of the ocean there rained down a large school which must have numbered several thousand. These came so quickly, so compactly, and flared into brilliance so suddenly that I instinctively ducked when they hit the aura of the light. For yards around the sea was packed with their close-set bodies. Most beautifully, they were swimming as one fish, veering and turning together, a great pink and lavender wheel that circled round and round.

Unfortunately their circling did not last for long, for like javelins out of the night a group of small hound-fish burst through the school, snapping and gulping their prey as fast as they could swallow. The anchovies scattered in all directions and for several minutes the water was streaked with lines of flashing colour which marked the trail of the fleeing fishes.

4: Pressure Problems in the Depths

One of the reasons why it was formerly believed that no life could inhabit the ocean deeps was the intolerable pressure, increasing at the rate of 15 pounds on every square inch (or one atmosphere) for every 30 feet of descent. Even the incomparably knowledgeable and curious Beebe was profoundly disconcerted by the reactions of a Bermudan lobster, which he wrapped in cheesecloth and tied to the outside of his bathysphere before diving to 2,200 feet. At that depth it was subjected to an overall pressure of 8 tons. Yet when the sphere surfaced again the lobster was found to be even more vigorous than before the descent. Piccard was also intrigued by this problem of pressure and, before making his 4,000-foot dive to the bottom of the San Diego Trough, wrapped half a dozen hens' eggs in cotton and packed them in a porous plastic box which he strapped to the outside of the Trieste. Since water seeped in through the eggs' semi-porous shells, equalizing the pressure within and without, they did not break—just as a metal box retains its shape under the most extreme pressure, providing that its sides are perforated. Nature has solved the problem with her habitual ingenuity by permeating the tissues of marine organisms with fluids of the same pressure as that of the sea around them.

It is true that many, perhaps most, of the ocean's fauna, and especially the fish, are restricted to zones within certain ranges of tolerable pressures. Those in the abyss are unable to ascend to levels where pressures are considerably less, and surface fish are unable to descend into regions of very high pressure. Suspended in the midwaters, buoyed and weightless, the angler fish swim unaware of the rhythmic flow of tide and time. Some indeed are enveloped in skinlike layers of jelly, which increase their ability to float in their motionless environment. No night, no day, no seasons, no changes in temperature—what laws govern their spawnings and migrations? Although wind-raised waves do not normally ripple the stillness of the midwaters, and the most violent storm and wave movements are barely perceptible 200 feet below the surface, the depths to which such surface disturbances penetrate is related to the length between the crests of the waves, and extremely long waves are in fact felt in the abyss. How, one wonders, are fish affected by typhoons and tsunamis, those 300-foot-high seismic waves which erupt from the great trenches and roll across the Pacific from coast to coast?

However, the range of pressures tolerable to both individuals and species may be considerable. Some sea urchins, and also worms, exist at all levels down to 16,000 feet. The giant sunfish is often on the surface when it is calm, lying on its side, sucking the plankton. But when the sea is rough it sinks into the depths, where, in contrast to the habits of most other fish, its young live. And such midwater fish as the lantern fish and stomiatoids (dragonfish and viperfish), and also the zooplankton, which migrate vertically to the surface at night must experience relatively rapid pressure changes of up to 450 to 600 pounds per square inch.

It is generally accepted that a gas-filled swim-bladder located just below the backbone is the device that enables most bony fish to move slowly up and down within their levels of tolerable pressure, and also to swim or hover at one level or over the bottom without any expenditure of energy. Some French biologists have expressed doubts that the swim-bladder fulfills this function. However, when a fish swims downward the increase in pressure squeezes gas out of the bladder, increasing the fish's apparent weight and decreasing its buoyancy. When it swims upward the gas content of the bladder is increased, and a balance is maintained between the weight of the fish and the water it displaces. So long as these ascents and descents are not made too sharply there are no complications from pressure changes. But if fish are hauled up too rapidly in trawl nets from depths of a few thousand feet, the sudden decrease in pressure may cause the gas in their swim-bladders to expand so rapidly that the bladders are forced out through their mouths. Bodies are distorted, scales wrenched off, eyes driven out of their sockets. Those fish without swim-bladders, though able to withstand pressures of 100 atmospheres, or 1,500 pounds per square inch, are, if trawled up alive, unable to swim at the surface because the lessened pressure blows them up like balloons, leaving them bobbing helplessly upside down.

Other forms of marine life also make use of gas to counteract the effects of pressure. The pearly nautilus, one of perhaps 650 species of cephalopods, which also include octopuses, squids and cuttlefish, lives in a shell with a maximum span of 10 inches. This contains from twenty-seven to thirty-six chambers and, as the nautilus grows, it moves from one chamber to another, sealing off each gas-filled chamber behind it. By varying the gas contents and pressure within the chambers it can rise or sink at will, while propelling itself through various depths down to 2,000 feet when hunting shrimps and bottom invertebrates.

The swim-bladders of some deep-living fish have apparently atrophied or have become filled with virtually incompressible fat, and the flatfish, mackerels, rays and some sharks never possessed them. In some species of sharks such as baskers and dogfish, their absence is compensated for by the presence in the immense livers (which may account for a quarter of the total body weight) of a particularly light

Pearly nautilus

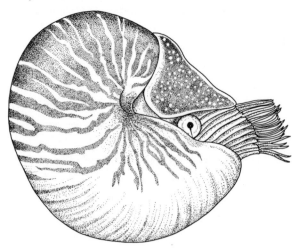

hydrocarbon, squalene, which renders them buoyant. A very few sharks, such as the gray nurse, improvise a hydrostatic organ by swallowing quantities of air, which they retain in their stomachs. There is a theory that the swim-bladder originated in freshwater fish as an auxiliary respiratory organ in waters deficient in oxygen, and was filled by air that the fish swallowed. But the majority of sharks must maintain buoyancy by the perpetual motion of their pectoral fins and the tail fin. If, without swim-bladders, they enjoy the advantage of being able to pass swiftly from one pressure level to another when hunting they are also at a disadvantage, as from birth to death they must swim continuously or sink to the bottom. They must also swim in order to breathe, because they obtain oxygen from the flow of water over their gills as they move forward. In contrast, most of the bony fish can

Pearly nautilus showing chambers

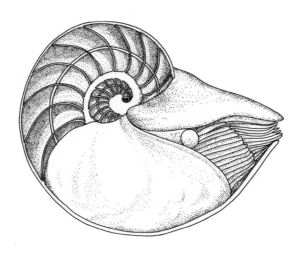

rest and breathe at a particular depth by pumping water in through their mouths and out over the gills, absorbing oxygen from the water during its passage over the latter. A sick shark in a tank will sink to the bottom and soon die from lack of oxygen if it is not "swum" round and round the tank by a diver. However, benthic or bottom-living sharks such as guitar fish, rays and skates, all of which can swim at a slow speed or rest on the bottom, are able to breathe by taking in water through vents on the top of the head and pumping a stream of water, regulated by valves, over the gills. Breathing by this method avoids clogging the delicate gills with sand or mud.

One may well ask how the ocean is adequately oxygenated. An obvious source is the phytoplankton. However, since photosynthesis diminishes with depth, there comes a stage when the phytoplankton becomes an exploiter instead of a producer, and supplies of oxygen diminish down to a depth of 1,500 feet. At that level they are replenished from cold currents. It was formerly believed that there were no currents in the abyss, and Piccard was surprised to find a half- or three-quarter-knot current flowing over the bottom of the San Diego Trough. But it is in fact the slow drift of these bottom currents, which advance at a rate of perhaps a mile a day, that carries the necessary oxygen to the deep fauna by transporting an immense volume of sinking polar water toward the equator. This water retains its original polar chill, its temperature remaining more or less uniform at 29 to 37 degrees F below 9,000 feet. The ocean-wide flow of these deep currents must be a primary factor in the distribution of the abyssal fauna and must account for the fact that the same species of some midwater invertebrates and even fish have been collected from seas as distant from one another as those off Greenland and South Africa. It has been proved that deep waters from the Arctic and Antarctic, and even from the Mediterranean, mingle in the Sargasso Sea, where there may exist a greater variety of midwater fauna than is present anywhere else in the ocean. The bristle worms and sea cucumbers in the bowels of one great ocean trench are identical with those in others, despite the vast distances separating them. It is more credible that their lowly progenitors were originally carried to their respective trenches by bottom currents than that they have evolved independently yet identically. Has Piccard's Challenger Deep "sole" identical relatives in other trenches?

The problem of how marine mammals counteract the effects of rapid and extreme changes of pressure during deep dives remains unsolved, though we have some evidence as to the depth and duration of their dives.

A bottle-nosed dolphin hunting for mullet normally sounds for about 15 minutes before surfacing to blow three or four times a minute; but a harnessed bottle-nosed dolphin has dived to a depth of 550 feet and up again in $2\frac{3}{4}$ minutes. Alaskan fur seals, with depth and time recorders strapped to their backs, reached depths approaching 1,500 feet during the course of dives with a maximum duration of 28 minutes, and one Weddell seal made fifty successive dives to a depth of 1,000 feet below the Antarctic ice, cruising from one ice-hole to another during the course of a dive. Another reached a depth of almost 2,000 feet during a 43-minute dive. We do not know what depths are reached by blue whales and bowheads during maximum sounds of 50 or 60 minutes, nor why these baleen whales should undertake such deep dives, for though some krill are to be found as deep as 3,000 feet, the mass are concentrated in the upper 30 feet. In this respect it may be relevant to note that about the only information available concerning the 20-foot pygmy right whale, other than that it is an inhabitant of the southern ocean, is that it possesses a greater number of ribs than any other whale. Since these become increasingly broadened and flattened toward the tail and are loosely attached to the backbone, they would provide almost complete protection for the whale's internal organs under pressure.

The deepest divers among the whales are the beaked whales and sperm whales, which may have to dive deep in order to search out their chief prey, the squids, which probably live mainly around the 3,000-foot level, below the twilight zone. Thirty-foot bottle-nosed whales have been recorded hunting squids at depths of 1,600 feet during 2-hour soundings, and sperm whales commonly sound for 40 or 50 minutes, with a maximum of an hour and a half. Both may also feed regularly on the sea bottom, for as many as ten thousand beaks of squid and octupuses have been taken from the stomach of a bottle-nose, and cuttlefish, octopuses, spiny lobsters, spider crabs and skates from those of harpooned sperm whales. It is possible that the dents that are often found in the foreheads of sperm whales could be caused by their striking the sea floor when searching for bottom food, for bowheads have been known to dive with such impetus in shallow waters as to break their jaws on the bottom. Squids, however, swallowed whole, are the sperm whale's main food, and it is their hard parrot-like beaks, together with the bony sucker-rings on their arms, that produce the fabulous ambergris, which is sometimes vomited by injured or harpooned whales. The presence in the intestines of more than half a ton of what is, alas, no more than hardened feces impacted around this dark and sticky matrix of indigestible matter, in no way incommodes a full-fed healthy whale, despite the gargantuan belchings and stomach rumblings of a school of sperm whale basking on the surface.

We have long known from the experiences of whalers that, while most sperm whales swim near the surface when harpooned, both they and beaked whales often dive to great depths. A beaked whale has been known to take 2,400 feet of line straight down, and harpooned sperm whales may dive with extraordinary speed and directness, taking several hundred fathoms of line vertically down in their power dives. One, indeed, struck by Prince Albert of Monaco, pulled out 1,300 feet of line "with such a powerful speed that the fore part of the boat took fire." But the whalers' assertions that a whale has sounded vertically with so many hundred feet of line may not take account of the fact that a quantity of line has been taken out at an angle, and the actual depth reached by the whale may thus have been overestimated. However, experiments with harpoons to which sounding tubes were attached proved that fin whales dived to depths varying from 276 to 1,164 feet and could tow a whaleboat for half an hour after sounding. Not until 1931, however, was a sperm whale's diving capability fully realized, when a 45-foot adult bull was found entangled in a submarine cable at a depth of 3,240 feet. There are now known to have been at least fourteen instances of sperm whales fouling cables on the sea floor, of which ten were off the Pacific coast of Central and South America. Six of these occurred at depths of between 2,700 and 3,360 feet, and one as deep as 3,720 feet. Since in the majority of cases the sperm whales had become entangled near sections of cable that had been broken and repaired, and the cable was wrapped around their lower

Sperm whale or cachalot

jaws, it is possible that they had fouled loops left slack during repairs and become further entangled during their struggles. Some were found with 180 feet of cable coiled around their bodies and tail flukes. Although all the cables had been severely lacerated by the whales' teeth and their insulation squeezed out, none were broken. A whale entangled in this manner would no doubt find it impossible to sever a cable's armor-wires, which have a breaking strength of between 8 and 20 tons; for its case is not comparable with that of a basking shark harpooned by Gavin Maxwell, which snapped a 3-inch manila rope with a breaking strength of 7 tons when sounding at full speed. To have fouled the cables the sperm whales must have been swimming at some speed, open-mouthed, along the sea floor. And it is reasonable to assume that they did not just swim accidentally into bights of the cables, but attacked them, perhaps mistaking them for the arms of large squids or octopuses.

No one, so far as I am aware, has been able to explain how sperm whales diving to submarine-cable depths, and no doubt deeper still, in a period of minutes can counteract pressure increases of more than 2,000 pounds on every square inch of their colossal bodies. It could be argued that their thick layer of blubber provides the same protection as the pressure-resistant hull of a submarine—but submarines don't open their mouths when they are submerged. As reasonable a theory as any is that the sperm whale is fitted with a hydro-static organ comparable to the swim-bladder of a fish, or, more realistically in regard to its size, the buoyancy tank of a submarine; for the greater part of its huge square-fronted head, one-third of its total body length, is a hollow tank filled with spermaceti—a spongy tissue impregnated with an extremely light viscous wax—lying in a deep layer at the bottom of a ton of light oil. It is significant that the head of a beaked whale also contains a reservoir of a substance very similar to spermaceti; though why a sperm whale's head should be completely asymmetrical, with the bones on one side of the upper jaw totally different from those on the other side, and its single blow-hole invariably located on the port side, is inexplicable.

An observation by Cousteau suggests a possibility that sperm whales sometimes dive so deep, or stay down so long when hunting squids, that they may almost exhaust their supply of oxygen. But we must not overstress the necessity for sperm whales to dive to great depths for their prey, for numerous forms of marine life, squids included, rise into the upper waters at night and can be hunted within a few score or hundred feet of the surface. However, it was in the late fifties that Cousteau's research ship encountered a scattered herd of about a hundred sperm whales at a locality in the Indian Ocean only ten miles from the scene of a similar meet-ing the previous year. From time to time the sea erupted with the high geysers of whales leaping vertically and clearing the water by 15 feet before falling back on their sides, and he estimated that they had come up from the deeps at such speed that they breached at 20 to 25 knots, as if in urgent need of oxygen.

This raises the further problem of how whales are able to make rapid ascents from deep dives without being affected by caisson sickness, the painful and potentially fatal bends that cripple the human diver when he surfaces too swiftly from dives and the nitrogen in his bloodstream becomes gaseous with the sudden lessening of pressure, clogging his veins and damaging his internal organs. A number of exotic, though not necessarily impossible theories have been advanced in explanation of the whale's immunity. In the case of baleen whales it is suggested that an oily foam in their respiratory system absorbs nitrogen when the lungs contract on diving and prevents it from entering the bloodstream; or that, because nitrogen is much more soluble in fats than in water, it is partially absorbed by the whale's enormous mass of blubber. A similar function might be served by the spermaceti in a sperm whale's head tank.

However, there could be a more practical explanation for the whale's immunity. Unlike the human aqualung diver, who is constantly breathing unlimited quantities of compressed air, a whale sounds with only the supply of air in its lungs—as does a marine turtle, whose plastron or ventral plates are fitted with a hinge that allows its chest to expand when its lungs are being filled with sufficient air for a 10-minute dive to a depth of at least 130 feet. Moreover, a whale's lungs are very thoroughly ventilated by a succession of blows or exhalations, when 90 per cent of its blood is reoxygenated. During the course of a succession of dives a sperm whale, for example, blows brief jets every 10 seconds or so for 10 or 15 minutes while lying just beneath the surface; while in similar conditions a blue whale blows a dozen times at 2-minute intervals, surfacing, blowing and submerging again in 30 seconds, before ultimately sounding for periods of from 10 to 30 minutes. This prolonged ventilation of a whale's lungs ensures that it dives with a minimum of nitrogen to be dissolved in its blood and tissues, while at the same time almost all the gas is forced out of its lungs by the increasing pressure of the water, still further reducing the amount of nitrogen that can be released into the blood-stream. Significantly, the proportion of nitrogen is least in those whales that are known to dive deepest, and their muscles also carry large amounts of myoglobin to assist the hemoglobin in the blood in building up reserves of oxygen. They are also able to conserve oxygen when diving, by a drastic and abrupt slowing of the heartbeat rate and consequent reduction in the circulatory rate of the blood.

5: Animal Lights in the
Black Abyss

It was long believed that all the inhabitants of the ocean below 2,500 or 3,000 feet lived in a world of eternal Stygian blackness, unrelieved by any trace of natural light. Only those that rose to feed in the upper waters during the earth's night could escape from this perpetual darkness. To Hans Hass, nevertheless, the sun was always shining in the blackest night of the deepest deep. For does not seaweed on the surface capture sunlight? And do not fish then swim up to nibble at the weed, consuming the energy it has captured from the sun, and are themselves devoured by other fish, which swim down into everlasting darkness as carriers of concentrated light?

But while it is true that there is no trace of natural light in the abyss, for photographic plates exposed for as long as 2 hours at 12,000 feet remain blank, there are clues that the darkness is not total. On the contrary, where there is life there is light, and throughout the ocean deeps there are zones of almost continuous light. By the most marvelously beautiful, though often unbelievably grotesque adaptations, the fish, squids, shrimps, prawns and plankton provide their own illumination in the darkness. It is a cold radiation, comparable to that emanating from luminous paint rather than from electricity. In a few seconds Beebe observed through the porthole of his bathysphere in the Sargasso deeps fifty different lights, the majority pale yellow, a few bluish. And frequently "the abundance of lights was so great that the comparison was unavoidable with the major stars on a clear moonlight night." Although those biologists who suggest that 90 per cent of the animals below 2,500 feet lighten the darkness with an almost continuous display of flashing pyrotechnics may exaggerate actual conditions, there are some grounds for their assertion.

Probably between one-third and one-half of all midwater and bottom fish, squids and lesser fauna are equipped with organs, called photophores, that emit light. Indeed, more than 96 per cent of the 115,000 fish which Beebe caught at depths down to 13,000 feet in Bermudan waters were equipped with them. Naturally, the optimum concentration of lights occurs where there is the greatest amount of life, and this is found in the twilight zone between 750 and 2,500 feet, whether in the oceans or in lesser seas such as the Mediterranean. At 900 feet a sensitive light-meter may register more light at night from this animal bioluminescence than from sunlight during the day, and the light may equal the intensity of sunlight at around 2,500 feet, with individual flashes a thousand times brighter. Even at depths of more than 6,000 feet the photomultiplier tube of Cousteau's *Calypso* registered flashes of light at intervals of just over 2 seconds in the least-

populated area; and this instrument also detected flashes
down to almost 12,000 feet.

Lilac, purple-orange, yellow, yellow-green, blue-green—
the variety of colors and patterns of colors is marvelous and
infinite. Almost seventy years ago the German marine
biologist Carl Chun first described the small diadem squid of
the Indian ocean: "One would think the body was adorned
with a diadem of brilliant gems. The middle organs of the
eye shone with ultramarine blue, the lateral ones with a
pearly sheen. Those towards the front of the lower surface
of the body gave out a ruby-red light, while those behind
were snow-white or pearly, except the median one, which
was sky-blue." Some fish also display different-colored lights.
One of the lantern fish is illuminated by an upper row of
red, blue and violet lights and a lower row of red and orange
lights, while its tail emits red lights only. The globular body
of a previously unknown fish, the most beautiful Beebe saw
from his bathysphere, was pricked out with lines of golden-
yellow lights, each partly or wholly surrounded by purple
lamps. He named it the five-lined constellation fish.

This submarine bioluminescence is a phenomenon distinct
from the phosphorescence exhibited on the surface of the
sea by fish and other floating objects reflecting the luminescence of the myriads of floating animalcules and plants—
algae, dinoflagellates such as *Noctiluca*, and the transparent
gooseberry-shaped ctenophores or comb jellies, jellyfish-like
organisms whose intense green lights glow over miles of sea
at night and are emitted in sudden flashes when a ship
cleaves through their multitudes. Sir Alister Hardy has
described how one August night, south of the equator, all
the surface of the sea was illumined by countless spontaneous
flashes of remarkable brilliance from comb jellies. Although

the flashes were of only a second or two's duration, each lit up the water for several feet around, and with hundreds igniting simultaneously, great flashes of light were produced, like rockets bursting under water.

Bioluminescence is a complex product basically involving a compound known as luciferin, which emits light when oxidized in the presence of an enzyme, luciferase. And there are three main types of photophores connected to the masses of light-producing cells by nerve "switches." The first type, possessed by polychaete or bristle worms and some fish, squids and bivalve mollusks, produces light outside the cells.

Polychaete worm

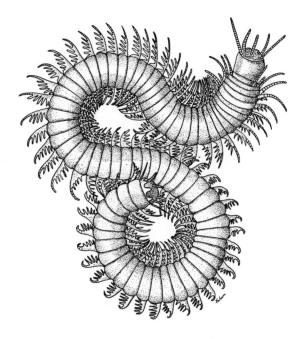

In the second type the light is produced within the cells situated in the liver or digestive gland of, for example, some deep-water shrimps, and shines through the animal's translucent skin, though in most midwater squids, prawns, and fish this type of cell-lighting is reflected forward by a silvery backcloth and focused through a lens-type thickening of the scale overlying the photophore. In the third type luminous bacteria are housed in a special sac in the photophore, and many kinds of squids have a pair of these bacterial photophores embedded in the ink sac. In fish they may be situated in such incongruous places as the lower jaw, the intestines, the wall of the esophagus or the ventral body-wall, and when deep-seated their glow is diffused widely over the body. In some of the deep-living squids they are actually located on the walls of the eyes, which are themselves situated on the ends of long stalks. In this case the surface of each photophore is covered with a layer of transparent pigmented cells, which enable the squid to vary the color of the light it emits. One must admit, however, that in some instances nature has one baffled. In two of the deep-living squids, for example, *Histioteuthis* and *Calliteuthis*, not only is the left eye approximately four times the size of the right, but the photophores are included in this asymmetry, for while the socket of the small heart-shaped right eye is surrounded by a well-developed circlet of photophores, those around the left eye are widely separated and distorted, and in some instances rudimentary or absent. One must agree with one biologist that it is impossible to conceive of any cause or purpose in this grotesque asymmetry, which must render it physically impossible for the animal to propel itself in a straight path without recourse to spiral movement or violent counter-twisting; for it would be far-fetched to suppose that the small eye functions in surface waters and the large eye in the dim light of the lower twilight zone.

Although bacterial photophores shine continuously, those of some animals are fitted with screening devices. A squid's may be masked by the pigment in its ink sac, while one species of fish, whose photophores are situated in the region of its cheek, can rotate them to conceal their light. Prolonged illumination by the two other types of photophores appears to be mainly chemically controlled, for the photophores light up if their owner is injected with adrenalin. But the majority of animals equipped with photophores emit light only intermittently, either spontaneously or in response to some external stimulus such as a touch or a pulse of light from another animal, and flash for relatively short periods. Light produced inside the cells of small shrimps shines for a maximum period of 20 seconds. That produced outside, for only a few seconds in fish, squids, prawns and copepods, and for a maximum of 5 minutes in one of the paddle worms.

However, bioluminescence is very efficient, since none of its energy is dissipated as heat; and the tenacity of the fragile organisms of the abyss is astounding, for some prawns brought up from a depth of 5,000 feet by Beebe not only lived and swam about in a dish for 2 hours but discharged barrages from their luminescent batteries that lit up the whole of the *Arcturus's* darkroom.

What purposes are served by these marvelous constellations of lights and patterns of lights? Some, no doubt, are merely fortuitous by-products of chemical processes or metabolic waste. But since several hundred fish, one squid in three, and hosts of lesser animals, including the zooplankton, are equipped with photophores, one must assume that the majority of these lights serve specific purposes. And if this is the case, then there must be eyes to see the lights. Piccard's flatfish in the ultimate deep possessed eyes, and, considering the total absence of light in four-fifths of the ocean's waters, it is highly significant that fish without eyes are almost unknown. Even those with degenerate eyes, such as some of the brotulids, are very few in number and probably confined to those that locate their food in the bottom ooze by feelers and thus have little use for sight. It appears to be widely believed that comparatively few animals inhabiting depths below 8,000 feet possess photophores. It is true that many of these abyssal fish—notably the brotulids—have smaller eyes than those inhabiting the twilight zone. On the other hand, some of the rattails living at least as deep as 13,000 feet have exceptionally large and sensitive eyes, which must be used solely for detecting animal lights. The latter may penetrate the darkness for a maximum distance of perhaps 100 feet, though it has been suggested that the green light emitted by a species of prawn may be three times as strong as this.

That most of the fish in the twilight zone have large and sensitive eyes is understandable, for they will require these when they migrate into upper waters at night. Their visual performance is improved by an increase in the rods that help the retina to pick up the dimmest light, and by the corresponding absence of the color-perceptive cells. It is further improved by the addition of golden pigments sensitive to the blue light prevailing in the twilight zone. In many cases the eyes point upwards, as those of the diminutive 2-inch-long hatchet fish do, or they are located on stalks and therefore perhaps are telescopic and enable their owners to focus more precisely on nearby objects or on the light-patterns of illuminated prey or predators. But quite apart from the obvious—that eyes would be redundant in the total darkness of the abyss if there were no animal lights on which to focus —one has also to remember that eyes cannot be employed for long-range vision in the twilight zone and above because maximum visibility, even in surface waters, is normally not more than 60 to 80 feet. And sight under water is comparatively unimportant, because fish and other forms of marine life are equipped with a variety of other sensory aids.

There is another aspect of underwater vision to consider. The pigment cells of various forms of marine life are apparently affected by the gradual diminution in the amount of natural light as depths increase. In the upper 600 feet some shrimps are pure white in color, but they are pinkish-white or pale pink throughout the next 900 feet and scarlet below that level. So too, while fish in the surface waters are predominantly bluish or colorless or even transparent, those between 600 and 1,500 feet are silvery, grayish or light brown. And though below these levels all fish are dark brown, deep violet or black, the commonest color among other creatures trawled to the surface is red—blood-red squids, bright red jellyfish, crimson prawns, scarlet or purple worms, reddish copepods. These are surely the most astounding hues to color a world in which there is no natural light to reveal them. It could be argued that in the twilight zone these brilliant colors are in fact those that reflect very little blue light either from the spectrum or from the bioluminescent lights of almost the same wavelength emitted by predators, and could therefore be considered as protectively concealing colors. But since the retinas of all or the majority of fish in this zone lack cones, the fish must be color-blind, and red would therefore presumably appear to them as no more distinctive than one shade of gray among many. Below the twilight zone, red must necessarily appear black in the total darkness and is therefore neither advantageous nor disadvantageous to its possessor, whether prey or predator— many of the latter being themselves black or dark red— providing that neither is bioluminescent.

There has long been a craze among scientists for interpreting any peculiarity as the product of some cunning evolutionary purpose. But in fact fish tend to produce black pigment or melavin more commonly than red, whereas crustaceans produce red pigment or carotenoid more commonly than black. The red pigment of many deep-living prawns, such as *Notostomus* (which is also reported to spawn red eggs), is deposited in its outer shell, the exoskeleton, but is lost when the prawn molts. This showy pigmentation could therefore be regarded as the accidental result of metabolic waste being stored in the outer shell. This is only a possibility, because in other crustaceans, such as the half-red prawn *Oplophorus*, the pigment is deposited below the outer shell and is therefore not lost during the molt.

In pondering this problem of incongruously showy coloring in utter darkness one recalls that crustaceans in the underground waters of terrestrial caves are invariably a pallid white, the eyes of many are atrophied, and there is no bioluminescent light in cave waters. If, therefore, red, *per se*, has any significance in the deep sea, it must be that of concealment against the lights of predators or to conceal the latter from the searching lights of their prey. Because some deep-living fish with well-developed eyes emit no lights with which to see with their eyes, while others emit brilliant lights but have too poor vision to see any objects the light may reveal, it has been argued that there is no correlation between

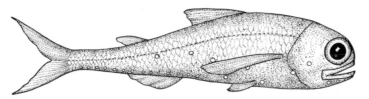

Lantern fish

lights and visual powers. But this argument misses the point, which is, of course, that one kind of fish has eyes in order to see the lights of other fish as prey or predator, and the other exhibits lights in order to attract prey or mate or the other members of the shoal. And we know that in fact the eyes of lantern fish and euphausiid shrimp are sensitive to the lights of the photophores of their own kind. Similarly, the few truly blind fish employ lights in order to lure prey or mate within reach of their other forms of sensory equipment, such as tactile feelers, or numerous elongated rays, which have evolved from pectoral fins.

There are other practical purposes served by photophores. Distinctive patterns could advertise their owners as dangerous or impalatable. Lights could dazzle, frighten away or confuse predators, as in the case of a polynoid worm that casts off flashing scales, which continue to flash repetitively, deflecting a predator from the worm's body while it crawls away. This technique is improved upon by another marine worm *Acholoe*. If this worm is bitten in two, its hind end continues to gleam brightly, riveting the attention of its attacker, while its unillumined forepart, which contains the main organs, swims away and later regenerates another hind end. Shrimps, minute crustaceans, squids and fish alike may discharge bright luminous clouds, under cover of which they can make their escape. The thumbnail-sized sepioid *Heteroteuthis dispar*, a cephalopod netted at depths of around 600 feet, can discharge a fiery mass instead of the normal squid-family cloud of ink, thus creating as much confusion for a predator and as efficient protection for itself as the emission of brown or black ink in sunlit waters. Ulric Dahlgren has described how *Heteroteuthis*

> . . . throws out of its syphon several little masses of mucus, which show no light at the moment of ejection, but almost instantly, as the oxygen of the water begins to work on them show a number of rod-shaped particles of a brilliantly luminous matter embedded throughout the very delicate mass. As the mass continues to expand, this light continues to grow brightly for as much as three to five minutes, after which it rather suddenly dies out.

One searsid fish discharges a myriad blue-green sparks from a sac in its shoulder, and the *Oplophorus* prawn emits a brilliant luminous cloud from a gland on the underside of its thorax when flicking itself backward from the rush of a predator. Another brilliant scarlet prawn can envelop itself in a glowing cloud of luminous matter ejected from a pore under each eye.

Beebe has pointed out that two kinds of defense clouds are emitted by abyssal prawns. One diffuses instantly into a glowing mist. The other explodes into a burst of individual sparks resembling the display of a diminutive Roman candle. The latter has a most startling effect and was the invariable reaction of prawns that collided with his bathysphere.

Conversely, predators may use their lights to illuminate prey. Some kinds of lantern fish, all of which have large and sensitive eyes, are equipped with very large bluish-green head photophores, which throw a 12-inch beam and can function like a miner's lamp, as can the large photophores situated near the eyes of these predatory stomiatoids, the dragonfish and viperfish. In these instances a muscle attached to the photophore enables its owner to control the nature of its light and either project a steady beam or flash intermittently.

Dragonet or dragon fish

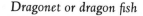

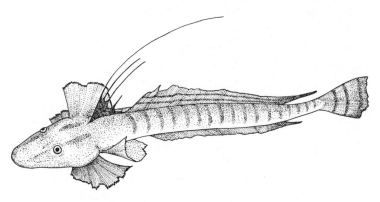

Another stomiatoid, an unidentified eel-shaped fish with two ocular photophores, has been observed feeding on krill near the edge of the pack-ice. Positioned from 2 to 6 feet below the surface, it emitted a beam of strong blue light, varying in intensity, which shone directly forward and partly upward for a distance of about 24 inches and illuminated the cloud of krill above, at which it snapped quickly from time to time. The krill are themselves equipped with photophores which flash brilliantly with a bluish-white beam and synchronize with the movements of their eyes to illuminate their smaller prey. The strip-lighting emitted by the millions of luminous bacteria housed in an open gland along the belly of a rattail may enable it to see the prey it has previously located by smell or touch, or which has perhaps been attracted by its lights; just as copepods and other zooplankton are apparently attracted to the solid sheet of light cast downward by the thirty-two photophores extending along the belly of one of the lantern fish. The latter in their turn are the prey of squids equipped with from twenty to as many as a hundred photophores, either spread over almost the whole of their bodies or restricted to the tips of their arms.

Beebe enjoyed the unique experience of watching a previously unknown squid, with luminous white spots painted on the irises of its enormous eyes and two orange bull's-eye lamps on the tips of its tentacles, catching lantern fish. His comment on this orange-lighted finger-squid, as he named it, was that "its life equipment is unsurpassed as regards eyesight, great speed, deadly suckers, and muscular arms." By jigging the photophores on the tips of its extremely long tentacles up and down like a fisherman hand-lining, another squid, *Chiroteuthis*, probably lures zooplankton within reach of the hooked suckers on its arms. But the fishermen of the abyss *par excellence* are the stomiatoids and angler fish, with luminous tassels, whips, bulbs, streamers or chin-barbels serving as lures. Even their appalling teeth may be luminous. One of the gulpers is equipped with a reddish photophore at the end of its whip-tail, whose glow no doubt attracts prey, for a specimen has been hauled up with its tail still wrapped round a small fish. Some angler fish, only a few inches long though with a girth equal to their length,

possess fantastically convoluting barbels, which are apparently the rays of dorsal fins transplanted to their foreheads
and are ten times the length of their bodies. But their barbels
can be used not only as lures but as sensory indicators of
potential prey, for Beebe observed that the slightest disturbance in the water near a black dragonfish's luminous barbel
"goaded it to the utmost so that it thrashed about and
snapped, striving to reach the source of irritation. Again
and again we proved the astounding sensitiveness of this
organ." So too, the bizarre seaweed-like growths below the
jaws of some angler fish may also contain sensory cells
apprising them of the approach of prey lured by the stalked
lantern on their foreheads.

An unusually large black angler fish, *Galatheathaume*
axeli, 19 inches long, trawled from a depth of almost 12,000
feet in waters west of Central America, is equipped with a
large forked photophore suspended from the roof of its mouth
and behind the curved and pointed teeth that fringe its
upper jaw like the rakers of a comb. Another deep-sea angler
has a long slender black rod, evolved from a spine, protruding forward from its head to just above its mouth, and a
lantern-like photophore at its tip twitches and winks. But
artificial baits are not restricted to deep-water angler fish. The
large "fishing frog" fish which lives among the floating sargassum weed possesses a bait in the form of a branched fleshy
tentacle at the end of a flexible spine which, when not in
use, is laid back on its head with the bait coiled in a small
hollow. When angling, the "fishing frog" erects the spine
above its head and moves it back and forward, slightly
vibrating the tentacle. If a fish is attracted to this semblance
of a swimming or wriggling worm, the tentacle is flicked
away when the victim is an inch or so from it, the "fishing

frog's" large mouth suddenly gapes, and the prey is swept in with the onrush of water. The jaws snap together with a movement too rapid to see, and the victim's tail disappears through the firmly closed mouth, which is furnished with recurved teeth hinged in such a manner that they bend inward when pushed from the front but spring back into erect barbs when a captured fish struggles to escape. No one, so far as I am aware, has ever watched a deep-water angler fish at work, but one presumes that it employs a similar technique to that of the "fishing frog," first attracting a victim with its illuminated lure, and then siphoning it into its mouth.

Although there cannot be any doubt that the abyssal ꞌngler fish employ their luminous lures to attract prey, emitting brief gleams of pale yellow, yellow-green, blue-green or purple-orange succeeded by longer intervals of darkness, it is most disconcerting to learn that in all except two of the eighty or one hundred species these lures are restricted to the females. How do the males obtain their food? A partial answer to this query is to be found in the unbelievably ingenious solution that half a dozen species of angler fish have found to the problem of mating in an environment in which encounters with the opposite sex may be infrequent. In these circumstances it is the youngest males that will stand the greatest chance of finding mates because, as they grow older, their numbers will be progressively reduced by predators. The males of these particular anglers are minute in comparison with the females, which are from six to twenty-five times as large, and up to twenty thousand times as heavy, and have slightly tubular upward-pointing eyes. When he is ultimately successful in locating a female, who makes known her whereabouts by flashing short intermittent series

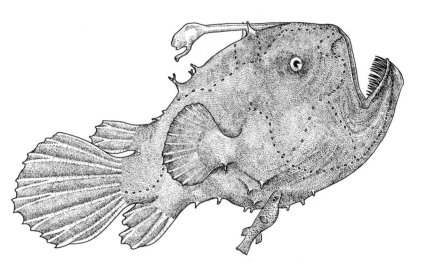

Angler fish with the dwarf male attached

of lights, varicolored according to her kind, from the bulbous photophore on her snout (and also perhaps, since the males are reported to possess the largest organs of smell of any vertebrate, by emitting some form of scent), the dwarf male grips the belly or head or gill-covers of her gigantic body with his jaws and continues to hold on to her until they actually become fused with her flesh, though he retains small openings on either side of the mouth for respiratory purposes. One 3-foot female may have three 6-inch males attached to her in this manner. The male then degenerates into a relatively enormous sexual organ and will for the remainder of his life be entirely dependent upon her blood and body fluids for nourishment, as compensation for fertilizing her eggs.

Some fish display sexually distinct patterns and positions of lights. The males emit brilliant flashes from extra-large platelike photophores on the upper side of the base of the tail; the females emit flashes from smaller photophores on the lower side. In other species the males shine their lights upward, the females downward. Possibly a mutual display of lights may stimulate and synchronize mating activities. Hans Hass once witnessed all the lights over an area of sea 150 or 200 feet in diameter flashing rhythmically with perfect synchronism—on for rather less than a second, off for $1\frac{1}{2}$ seconds.

We know that fireworms employ their lights as a means of sexual recognition, for when the females are ripe with eggs they rise from the coral reefs to the surface shortly after sunset, two or three nights after the full moon, and swim in small circles on the surface, emitting a glowing bright-green trail, to which the males, themselves flashing lights, are attracted. If no male responds to a female's signals, she switches off her lights temporarily. If she does this when a male is in fact approaching, the latter swims around aimlessly until she switches on again. Several males may be attracted to one female, and the whole group gyrates in a fiery circle while eggs and sperm are emitted simultaneously. But once this mating has been enacted, the lights of both sexes flicker out.

Serially arranged light patterns are so distinctive that they could serve as specific recognition signals and would be valuable to animals which, like the euphausiid shrimps, move in shoals or schools. The midshipman fish is, for example, illumined by a series of photophores aligned along its head and body, which light up progressively to resemble yellow portholes. Although there are more than two hundred kinds of lantern fish, all can be identified by the pattern of round pearly photophores studding their sides. Conversely, in the well-populated twilight zone distinctive patterns could be mutually repulsive, the intensity of light emitted and the distance at which it is visible being employed to demarcate hunting territories.

6: They Rise by Night

Vertical migration is a nightly phenomenon of the ocean. Zooplankton ascend to graze in the meadows of phytoplankton, and in pursuit of them come copepods, prawns, shrimps and other crustaceans, followed in their turn by fish and squids. The sheer number of organisms involved in this mass ascent staggers belief. On one dark moonless evening Beebe patiently calculated that after an hour's surface trawling at 2 knots with a silk net 3 feet in diameter he had collected just over 40 million individual planktonic copepods, snails and shrimps, together with their eggs. Yet on repeating this trawl under as nearly as possible the same conditions twelve hours later in full daylight, his catch numbered only about 1,000 individuals of the same groups.

Almost all the zooplankton take part in this nocturnal ascent, despite the fact that most of them have to climb from depths below 600 feet, and some from as far down as 1,500 feet. Among larger animals, some squids come up from depths below 2,500 feet. Different animals apparently ascend and descend at their own special times, for during the period of movement there is not a simultaneous rise en masse but a distribution in layers throughout the upper 600 or 1,000 feet, with concentrations at varying levels, associated perhaps with varying intensities of light. Many of the migrants are equipped with photophores, and in most cases, particularly in shrimps and fish, these shine downward, though the eyes are positioned to look upward. This being so, it has been suggested that the first migration creates an area of light that inhibits the upward movement of other animals below, thus bringing order into what would otherwise be confusion. These migrations must involve the minute plankton in extraordinary exertions and an immense output of energy during their many hours of climbing and sinking. One of the Antarctic *Euphausia* (a small shrimplike creature), for example, rises with remarkable speed from depths below 600 feet, and laboratory experiments have demonstrated the unexpectedly powerful swimming abilities of these tiny creatures. The rice-sized *Calanus* copepod can, for instance, climb at the rate of 50 feet an hour, and a Norwegian euphausian, 1 inch long, more than 300 feet an hour: the former swims down again 150 feet in the same period, and the latter 420 feet. Yet these are plankton, so named because they were considered helpless drifters at the whim of winds and currents. Clearly, this term is only truly applicable to those microscopic organisms unable to swim strongly enough to evade the ordinary plankton net.

There is no doubt that the primary purpose of this mass ascent throughout the ocean is to feed in those upper waters where the maximum sources of plant and animal food are concentrated. And it is presumably nocturnal because during

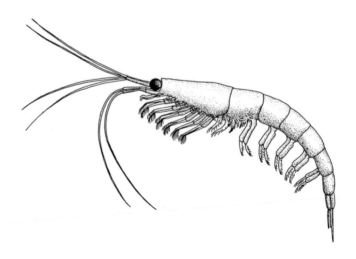

Euphausid

the earth's night the light in the upper waters is of approximately the same intensity as it is in deeper levels during daylight. It can hardly be argued that animals that are potential prey take advantage of the cover of darkness to come up to feed, because so many of them advertise their presence with photophores. The euphausians, for example, are brilliantly luminous. These migrations do not reach the actual surface waters on moonlight nights, and Cousteau has drawn attention to an interesting example of the effect of moonlight. The fishermen of Madeira are dependent for their living on a single species of deep-water fish, the predatory *espada*, which averages 10 pounds in weight and resembles a black, fiery-tinted barracuda with sabre teeth and enormous green eyes. For this fish they employ 5,000 feet of line baited with strips of squid on the lower 500 feet; but on moonlight nights they have to set their lines 1,500 feet deeper. However, if the moon becomes obscured by clouds they must haul the lines back to the normal 5,000-foot level in order to regain contact with the *espada*. Since the light of the moon cannot penetrate to such depths, the predatory *espada* is obviously responding to the up-and-down movements of its prey, which are themselves hunting other fish and plankton affected by the intensity of the moonlight in upper waters. Similarly, marine life in general, with certain inexplicable exceptions, inhabits deeper levels on days of bright sunshine than on cloudy days, when there are correspondingly more animals in surface waters.

On the surface of Cornish seas, as on other seas the world over, there is the miraculous beauty on calm nights of shimmering pools cast by the fishing smacks' clusters of light-globes. These, say the fishermen, attract the plankton and especially the crustaceans on which the fish feed, rather than the fish themselves. But this is not the whole truth, for though strongly diffused light, such as that cast by the moon, repels fish and plankton alike, all forms of bathypelagic life are invariably attracted to artificial surface lights. Immense shoals of squids gather at the surface at night and leap upward towards the lights used by oceanographers, and Johan Hjort has described how, when the crew of his research ship was hauling long lines on the Faroe slope and working by the light of an electric lamp hanging over the side, one squid after another would shoot like a flash of lightning toward it. Night after night young squids propelled themselves aboard the *Kon Tiki*, attracted by the light of the small paraffin lamp that served the raft as riding light, while the devilish green eyes of large squids floating on the surface gleamed like phosphorus. Night after night flying fish, large and small, landed on the raft. In fact, the Solomon Islanders catch flying fish by netting them as they "fly" into the glare of palm-leaf torches. Even when being hunted, flying fish are drawn to surface lights as if they may find escape in the illumination. As soon as a cluster of lights was lowered over the side of Beebe's *Arcturus*, large flying fish began coming in. "Never have I seen such uninterrupted terror or constant fear," wrote Beebe. "We could see nothing in pursuit . . . yet the flying fish dashed frantically about within the blaze of light. . . . We had to be on our guard, for they would strike with terrific force against our bodies and the side of the *Arcturus*." Twice in one week, once when it was overcast and pitch-dark and once when it was starlight, *Gempylus*, the bathypelagic snake mackerel, shot clean out of the sea and onto the *Kon Tiki*, actually knocking over the lamp on the first occasion. The fish was more than 3 feet in length, as attenuated as a snake, with a bluish-violet back and steel-blue belly, a long snout filled with sharp teeth, and huge black eyes. This was the first live *Gempylus* seen by man. That such a fish existed, supposedly at great depths, had previously been known only from the skeletal remains of a few specimens washed ashore on the coasts of South America and the Galápagos.

Underwater, the reactions to man's artificial lights vary. In deep water one fish was so startled by the floodlamps of Piccard's bathyscaphe, when it was resting on the bottom of the Mediterranean at a depth of 4,200 feet, that it buried itself in the mud. But another was apparently attracted, and hundreds of white isopod crustaceans collected in the cone of light. So too, at the same depth on the floor of the San Diego Trough, one sablefish swam into the light area and then rested peacefully on the bottom in the bright glow, while another attempted to enter the bathyscaphe's porthole. On

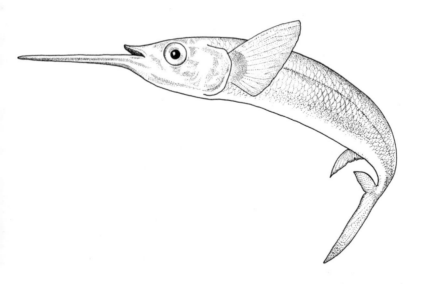

Ballyhoo halfbeak

the other hand, in much deeper waters the powerful search-light of Beebe's bathysphere failed to attract organisms of any kind, despite the fact that plankton were abundant. In upper waters Robert Schroeder found that his observations at night among the reefs of the Bahamas were greatly hampered by the fact that his artificial lights so confused, and also blinded, the fish and other fauna that they ceased all normal activities. Indeed, the stiletto beam of an ultrapowerful flash-light would hypnotize a fish into immobility. Yet Gilbert Klingel found that such fish as anchovies, silversides, half-beaks and menhaden, together with certain crustaceans and swimming worms, were irresistably attracted to his flashlight, but not to the tremendous glare of powerful electric lights. Worms in particular were stimulated to frenzy by the former:

Looping, undulating, vibrating, shaking and shivering, they whirled about the lens in a vermiform frenzy . . . a long body slithered along the curve of my forearm and burst into the light. . . . It was a brilliant worm of light scarlet fronted with a yellowish head, and it was being rowed along with several scores of triangular green oars composed of fibrous bristles. From its fantastic head covered with whisker-like blue cirri to its pointed, feathery tail it was about seven inches long. In the rays of the flash it shimmered and scintillated with iridescent light.

The galaxy of worms which had collected in front of my light were the forerunners of a considerable mass . . . intent on nothing but their interminable whirling about each other's bodies. I am convinced that they were in the throes of their reproductive cycle, for I noted that certain individuals were giving off exceedingly faint emanations, somewhat like smoke, which must have been either unfertilized ova or male sperm. When a newly advanced worm hit these miniature clouds it went into a blind frenzy which made its previous activity seem mild.

There is an odd aspect of this noctural migration. Since the surface currents of the ocean flow at different speeds and in different directions from those below 300 feet, a mass of plankton that has ascended at sunset will find itself a mile or so down-current at sunrise and will descend into a different part of the twilight zone the next day. Over a period of climbing and sinking it will move progressively farther down-current, and in this way there could be a perpetual dispersal of the plankton over the ocean meadows. This would also apply to the larvae and fry of all those bathypelagic species that begin life in the surface waters and would be carried considerable distances from their hatching places before

especially euphausians, or of the cast skins of small planktonic crustacea sinking through the depths—Cousteau's "great
bowls of living soup growing thicker the deeper into the
tureen we go." But if they are euphausians, they cannot be
krill, for the layers are rarely recorded in the Antarctic. And
there is a further objection to their being formed of any kind
of plankton. On one occasion in the Indian Ocean Cousteau's
Calypso detected a very thick trace of Deep Scattering Layers
at a depth of 400 feet. But when the camera was lowered to
this depth, the trace vanished from the echograph. Yet as the
camera was winched deeper, it reappeared. This particular
layer must therefore have been composed of organisms that
were not only densely packed but also swift-moving. Neither
plankton nor jellyfish fulfill the latter condition.

Although the mystery has still not been solved, there
would appear to be two possible origins of the Deep Scattering
Layers—small squids or small fish. In favor of these possibilities is a further observation by Cousteau that the Deep Scattering Layers sometimes break up into horizontal layers, as
if combined schools of a number of different species were
disintegrating and scattering, with each particular species
perhaps seeking the most agreeable level of light intensity.

Fish, it has been argued, are not admissible because nowhere
in the ocean are they to be found in shoals of such unprecedented size, except of course in limited spawning areas,
where shoals of herring have been estimated to aggregate 500
million to the square mile. That, so far as our knowledge goes,
is true. Nevertheless, small fish are extremely numerous in
the levels between 600 and 3,000 feet, and echograph smudges
of "gray angels," which are usually schools of fish including
hatchet fish, are frequently recorded from the twilight zone
in the Mediterranean. One should add that by the time a

beam from an echo-sounder has penetrated to a great depth it is blanketing a wide area, and any reflections from a large animal in this area would appear on the echograph as a dark, formless smudge or "black angel." But since no black angels have ever been recorded, it is possible that some deep-sea inhabitants, such as octupuses, are too acoustically "soft" to reflect ultra-sound effectively. There is a record of a knotted tangle of cable mixed up with a "fish," possibly an octopus, being hauled up from a depth of 7,200 feet some 30 miles off the coast of Portugal; and an abyssal octopus, *Grimpoteuthis*, with remains of benthic crustaceans in its stomach, has been trawled up from almost 15,000 feet in the Weddell Sea. The more or less spherical body sacs of these abyssal octopuses are semitransparent and as soft and fragile as those of comb jellies. At least one species is blind and some, such as the very small but very terrible cephalopod *Vampyroteuthis infernalis*, neither true octopus nor true squid, are sooty black. Beebe's description of this sole survivor of relatives that lived in the Cretaceous era was "black as night, with ivory-white jaws, blood-red eyes, and eight cupped arms all joined by an ebony web."

The Deep Scattering Layers' echo is characteristic of a reflection from small gas bubbles, such as one might expect to receive from a fish's swim-bladder acting as a resonator with a strong echo, or possibly from the gas-filled chambers by means of which a nautilus rises and sinks. Swim-bladders are highly developed in many fish that undertake extensive vertical migrations, notably so in the lantern fish, which rise to the surface in such numbers that for five hours one night a weather ship steamed through their shoals; and also in the viperfish and great swallowers that prey on them. Special observations from an American diving saucer demonstrated

7: Out of the Unknown Ocean

On starlit nights even the exceedingly hard-bitten members of the *Kon Tiki's* crew were aware of fear when two round shining eyes would suddenly rise out of the phosphorescent sea right alongside the raft and glare at them with an unblinking hypnotic stare. There were also the shining eyes of unknown fish risen from the deeps and drawn to the glimmer of the mastlight. There were balls of light, 3 feet or more in diameter, flashing at irregular intervals from assemblies of unknown animals; and "several times, when the sea was calm, the black water round the raft was suddenly full of round heads, 2 or 3 feet in diameter, lying motionless and staring at us with great glowing eyes."

Who can say what animals, never previously seen by man, remain to be discovered in the abyss? No doubt the majority of these are small, only a few inches in length, like most of the inhabitants of the deeps; though we should not overlook the fact that until the thirties of this century fewer than a hundred specimens of such a monstrous creature as the whale shark had been recorded in the annals of science, despite the facts that this shark had long been well known to the native fishermen of the Pacific and that Beebe saw eleven different individuals in the space of four days off Baja California. Even in the relatively restricted area of British coastal seas, the 14-foot false killer whale was known only as a subfossil skeleton from the Cambridgeshire fens until 1927, when a herd of 150 was stranded on the shores of the Dornoch Firth. There must be numbers of cetaceans of whose existence we are aware only from fewer than half a dozen specimens cast up on the world's beaches. As recently as 1938 four whales, the largest 30 feet in length, of an entirely new species were stranded on a New Zealand beach.

Paradoxically, the chances of sighting a large marine animal are less now than they were in the last century, for the changeover from sail to power has meant that almost all oceanic shipping is restricted to relatively narrow sea-lanes, from which many fish and mammals may well be driven by the painful vibrations of powerful engines, and immense areas are never visited from one year to the next. But we do not need to explore uncharted seas to plumb the depths of our ignorance of the ocean's less obvious inhabitants. During the winter, for example, four million fur seals fish off California. They feed, however, not to any extent on the known commercial varieties of fish, but on one belonging to a group that lives typically in very deep waters off the edge of the continental slope. Yet this fish is known only from the bones found in the seals' stomachs and has never been seen alive.

We have only to recall the "miracle" of the coelacanth, which on a December day in 1938 was trawled from a bottom of only 220 feet off East London on the east coast of South Africa, to realize how little we know of life below the ocean's surface. Here was a large carnivorous fish, 5 feet long and 127 pounds in weight, of a luminous dark blue characteristic of inhabitants of the twilight zone. Yet before that day the coelacanth was apparently known to science only as a "fossil" (with which it proved to be identical) in rocks laid down in the Cretaceous era, sixty to seventy million years ago. In 1952, again in December, a second coelacanth was obtained off the Comoro Islands northwest of Madagascar and some two thousand miles to the north of East London. And during the next two years a further six were caught at night by hook and line off the Comoros at depths of between 450 and 1,200 feet. Some of these had probably risen from greater depths in pursuit of nocturally ascending prey. One, hauled up alive at moonrise from 840 feet, survived for $17\frac{1}{2}$ hours in a covered whaleboat, until the following afternoon, when it died from the effects of what has been variously described as decompression, sensitivity to light, or exposure to warm water—possibly the latter mainly, since the surface waters in the Mozambique Channel are nearly 50 degrees warmer than those in the depths.

The miracle of the coelacanth will no doubt be repeated again and again, for the Comoro Islanders have in fact long known of it as the *kombessa*, and are so familiar with it as to use its rough scales as an abrasive when repairing bicycle tires. But though some coelacanths are dried and salted by the Comoro Islanders, they are not considered very good eating. There may be coelacanths in other seas, for in 1964 a 4-inch silver model of one, believed to date from the early 1800s, was discovered hanging in a village church near Bilbao, a few miles inland from the Bay of Biscay. Accurately proportioned to scale, it must have been modeled on a live or recently dead specimen.

In 1965 another previously unknown bathypelagic fish was washed up on a Natal beach and duly recorded by Professor J. L. Smith, who had been associated with the discovery of the first coelacanth. The following year Paul Tzimoulis, editor of *Skin Diver*, sighted yet another unknown when diving at a reported depth of 4,000 feet in the San Diego Trough. This was an immense fish, some 25 feet in length and 5 or 6 feet in diameter, with eyes about 6 inches across. A mottled brown in color with grayish-white tips to its scales, fins and tail, it somewhat resembled a coelacanth.

Photographs of a fish, possibly a shark, between twenty and thirty feet in length, have been taken at a depth of more than 6,000 feet off southern California, and there must be numbers of unknown species of sharks in the deeps. Frilled sharks, which have many anatomical resemblances to primitive forms of sharks that existed twenty-five or thirty million years ago, are occasionally caught at depths of between 1,200 and 2,750 feet in seas as far apart as those of Japan, California and the British Isles. There is therefore no reason why the giant shark, *Carcharadon megalodon*, may not still survive. Indeed, it would be a much more likely survivor than the coelacanth, for the manganese deposits on the teeth of this shark, dredged up from the red clay bottom at depths approaching 15,000 feet in the South Pacific, suggest that their owners may still have been in existence after the last of the ice ages; and since that era there have been no cataclysmic or climatic changes, with the possible exception of submarine volcanic activity, that could have fundamentally affected life in the ocean deeps. *Megalodon* probably belonged, or belongs, to the same genus as the great white shark, which still survives in warmer seas throughout the world and is itself a fearsome creature reaching lengths of more than thirty-six feet. Armed with appalling serrated and triangular teeth 2½ inches high, the latter can chop up an animal as large as a sea lion. Since the *Megalodon* teeth recovered were more than twice this size, it has been asserted that this monster must have been at least 90 feet long; but direct arithmetical comparison cannot be considered valid, and *Megalodon* could have been smaller or larger than this—larger, perhaps, than a blue whale. However, since the skeletons of sharks are composed of cartilage or gristle instead of bone and therefore decompose almost as rapidly as their flesh, only the direct capture or early location of a beached carcass can provide definite proof of *Megalodon*'s survival.

Regarding this possibility, one might ask, with Michael Tweedie, what carnivore controls the numbers of the giant squid *Architeuthis*, the semimythical *kraken* of the Norwegians, which has fascinated sailors and fishermen and infuriated credulous and incredulous zoologists for centuries. To preserve the ecological balance there ought to be a very large predator capable of preying upon these colossal, powerfully armed cephalopods. But so far as we know they are hunted in the world's oceans only by the few hundred thousand sperm whales. Would these exercise an adequate control? *Architeuthis*, it must be stressed, is not the sperm whales' only prey, nor possibly their main prey, for large numbers of medium-sized squids are certainly taken by them —though not, one fancies, enticed by the whale's purple tongue and white lips into its open mouth, as is asserted in one authoritative study. A mouth all the colors of the rainbow would blush unseen in the depths frequented by hunting sperm whales. As many as 28,000 small squids have been taken from the stomach of one sperm whale and 576 pounds'

Common octopus

weight from that of another; while the largest of 112 squids of at least 8 different species, taken from the stomachs of 39 sperm whales harpooned off the Azores, did not exceed 8 feet and averaged only 3 feet. Various kinds of fish, mainly deep-water, including large angler fish and such bottom-dwellers as skates and octopuses, but also albacores, barracudas, and sharks, including a young 8-foot basking shark and an entire 10-foot black-tipped shark, have also been recorded as prey and may perhaps amount to as much as 10 per cent of a sperm whale's food. There may well therefore be need for additional predators such as *Megalodon*.

Few sharks, however, except the primitive frilled sharks, prey extensively on squid, though blue sharks gorge on their mating assemblies. Their fearful batteries of teeth are for shearing and cutting when the undershot lower jaw is protruded, whereas a sperm whale's forty to sixty huge peglike teeth, each 8 inches high and more than 2 pounds in weight, which clamp into sockets in the immensely tough horny tissue lining the toothless upper jaw, are generally considered, probably correctly, as perfectly designed for seizing and gripping large slippery objects such as squids. Nevertheless immature sperm whales, whose teeth do not even erupt until they are nine or ten years old, are also capable of securing squids of all sizes. There is no doubt, however, about a sperm whale's ability to capture and swallow whole the largest squid or other form of prey. Witness that 48-foot sperm whale harpooned off the Azores in 1955, whose stomach contained a complete and intact architeuthid weighing more than 400 pounds and measuring 34½ feet overall.

Nor is there any doubt about the reality of giant squids, though there is no evidence of the existence of giant octopuses. Although one species of Pacific octopus spans 32 feet, all except 18 inches of this measurement is contributed by its arms. Giant squids, however, have been seen on the surface of the sea and vomited by harpooned sperm whales. Rather than inhabiting the abyssal deeps they probably live mainly in the ultimate depths of the twilight zone, around 3,000 feet, where eyes with a diameter of as much as eighteen inches would be useful in the near-darkness for hunting the fish and fauna of the continental slope. If the eggs found by Hans Hass when skin-diving in the Indian Ocean, and also those washed up on a Jamaican beach, were spawned by an architeuthid and not by some other species of large squid, it seems unlikely that they can have floated up from a depth greater than 5,000 feet. The colossal aggregation of eggs (probably laid by a number of squids) encountered by Hass were housed in an almost transparent sausage-shaped jelly six feet long and twelve inches in diameter, fashioned in an endlessly coiled thread of innumerable tiny spheres arranged one behind another like beads, each of which contained the well-developed embryo of a squid. The firm, though elastic and slippery cylinder of jelly protected the eggs not only from fungoid growths but also from predators. Fish had not been able to nibble through it; sea anemones could not digest it; while even a starfish's corrosive digestive juices required seventy-two hours to do so. When the eggs hatched in the laboratory the following day, Hass observed that even at this early stage the squidlings were already in possession of the pigment cells that enable the adults to conduct their kaleidoscopic color changes.

Although squids are reported to attach their eggs to some object on the sea floor, the finding of these floating cylinders suggests that not all do so. However, whether they attach them or not, they have no further association with the eggs once they have been spawned. This behavior is in extraordinary contrast to that of octopuses, which care for their eggs with exhausting tenderness after depositing them in a bivalve shell or other suitable receptacle. Although the more than 180,000 eggs may take as long as sixteen weeks to hatch, the octopus never leaves them in order to feed during this period and constantly cleans them, removing every grain of sand with the acutely sensitive suction pads on her arms. Cephalopod eggs are susceptible to fungoid infection, and a captive octopus will lug her shellful of eggs to the side of an aquarium in order to oxygenate them with fresh water from the inflow. If Hass's observations on captive octopuses are typical, the female assists the young ones to hatch out with

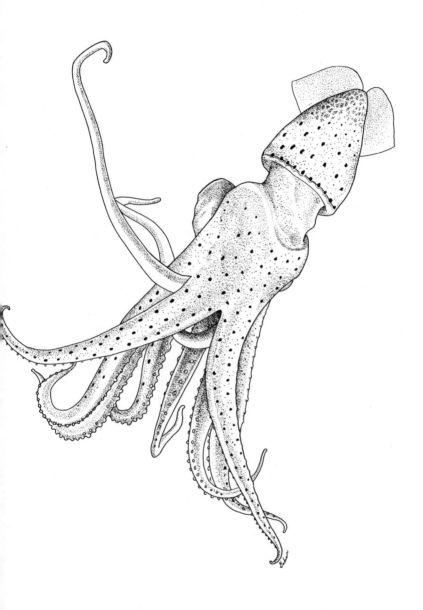

Squid

her suction pads and hurls them upward with expulsions of air from her breathing tubes. After all have hatched, she dies almost immediately, just as, in Pierre Labat's experience in Mediterranean waters, she eats the male after they have mated, fulfilling Saint Thomas's dictum that "Love is an appetite for oneness."

If the habits of the architeuthids resemble those of the Humboldt Current's large, but not giant, squid *Ommastrephes gigas*, which measures up to 12 feet in length and weighs 350 pounds, they are voracious hunters. By night and by day the *Gigas* squids slaughter the fish and also the sharks of the upper waters, taking a heavy toll of the tuna of the coastal fisheries and in particular of the 50-pound yellowfin tuna, of which they eat all except the head. Anything and everything edible is attacked, including those of their own kind which have been hooked by fishermen. All species and sizes of squids, from 2-inch specimens upward, are distinguished by their insatiable appetites and by their urge to kill in excess of their requirements. Immense schools of small squids may be driven by this impulse to kill and kill, taking only a bite here and there out of their victims, and in this frenzied hunting run themselves ashore on beaches in such numbers as to pile up in windrows more than a foot high.

A squid swims by siphoning water into its capacious body cavity or mantle and then, by powerful muscular contractions, forcing the water out in rapid jets through a funnel-like nozzle beneath the head. Streamlined from the arms shooting out in a cluster from its head to its torpedo-shaped mantle, it is propelled at high speeds. For instantaneous directional changes it relies on swift and powerful propellor-like strokes by two "winged" lobes of skin near the tail. These also act as stabilizers, and all cephalopods are further equipped with directional balancing organs (statocysts) in their heads—particularly complex in the speedy squids and particularly large in the free-ranging octopuses of the twilight zone. The nozzle can be pointed either forward or backward, and the squid is propelled in the opposite direction to that of the water jets. When swimming at speed, it normally progresses backward, for since its very large mammal-like eyes are situated on the sides of its head it has a wide rearward field of vision, though it cannot see dead astern. Thus, if, in darting this way and that, in frenzied pursuit of a shoal of fish, it runs aground, it continues to pump water vigorously from the nozzle, directed seaward, forcing itself still farther aground, to die as the tide ebbs. Moreover, if thrown back into deeper water, it repeatedly and inexplicably shoots back again to the beach—cephalopodic suicide.

The power generated by a large squid's jets is tremendous. That of a stranded *Gigas* has been compared to the blast from a firehose, while an architeuthid, in its struggles to regain the sea after being stranded on a Newfoundland beach, "ploughed up a trench or furrow about thirty feet long and of considerable depth by the stream of water that it ejected with great force from its syphon." Another, stranded on an ebbing tide in Tickle Bay, Newfoundland, in November 1878, was "making desperate efforts to escape, and churning the water into foam by the motion of its immense arms and tail. From the funnel at the back of its head it was ejecting large volumes of water. At times the water from its syphon was as black as ink." Giant squids normally inhabit warm seas and, if migrating into colder ones, would tend to rise out of the deeps into warmer surface waters. Since the majority of stranded architeuthids have been wrecked after storms, with their stomachs invariably empty, on the shores of such northerly regions as Newfoundland, the British Isles and Scandinavia, the probability is that they have been too weakened by prolonged exposure to lower than tolerable temperatures to hunt for food. Some, however, have perhaps been injured in surface encounters with sperm whales and have not been able to migrate back to their native seas. None, strangely enough, have provided any evidence of being sexually mature. They apparently undertake extensive migrations, making use perhaps of deep currents and countercurrents still largely uncharted by oceanographers, for a school of sixty has been sighted off Newfoundland, and there is some evidence that they tend to visit the North Atlantic in large numbers at intervals of about thirty years.

Much of what knowledge we have of giant squids has been obtained circumstantially from sperm whales. Frank Bullen gave a graphic account in *The Cruise of the Cachelot* of a struggle between a sperm whale and a giant squid, which he witnessed at eleven o'clock one night at the entrance to the Malacca Straits:

> I was leaning over the rail, gazing steadily at the bright surface of the sea, when there was a violent commotion in the sea right where the moon's rays were concentrated, so great that . . . I was at first inclined to alarm all hands, for I had often heard of volcanic islands suddenly lifting their heads from the depths below, or disappearing in a moment. . . . Getting the night-glasses out of the scuttle . . . I focused them on the troubled spot. A very large sperm whale was locked in deadly conflict with a cuttle-fish, or squid, almost as large as himself, whose interminable tentacles seemed to enlace the whole of his great body. The head of the whale especially seemed a perfect network of writhing arms . . . for it appeared as if the whale had the tail of the mollusc in his jaws, and, in

a business-like, methodical way, was sawing through it. By the side of the black columnar head of the whale appeared the head of a great squid, as awful an object as one could well imagine, even in a fevered dream. Judging as carefully as possible, I estimated it to be at least as large as one of our pipes, which contained three hundred and fifty gallons; but it may have been, and probably was, a good deal larger. The eyes were very remarkable from their size and blackness, which, contrasted with the livid whiteness of the head, made their appearance all the more striking. They were, at least, a foot in diameter. . . . All round the combatants were numerous sharks . . . apparently assisting in the destruction of the huge cephalopod.

Bullen's account was confirmed in the 1950s by a French master mariner, who has described an encounter off the coast of Chile between a giant "octopus" and a 50-foot sperm whale, which was in the process of chewing off two of the cephalopod's tentacles, 25 or 30 feet in length, which were entwined around its head. And more recently Commander Arne Groenningsaeter of the Royal Norwegian Navy has reported how on three occasions between 1930 and 1933 the 15,000-ton motor vessel *Brunswick* was "attacked" by a giant squid when sailing between Hawaii and Samoa. In each instance the attacks were made in daylight and in good visibility, with the commander enjoying a perfect view from the vessel's bridge, 50 feet above the water. He estimated all three squids—or was it the same individual?—to be 30 feet or more in length. However, in addition to their eight arms, squids (and also cuttlefish) are equipped with two very much longer tentacles, which may be several times the length of the mantle and which terminate in a club-shaped swelling covered with closely set rows of suckers. When making a kill, a squid shoots out these tentacles and, clasping the fish with them, draws it back to the grasping arms. But since the tentacles are partially retracted when not in use, Groenningsaeter could well have underestimated the size of his squids, for the tentacles of a New Zealand specimen are reputed to have measured 49 feet 3 inches of its overall length of 57 feet.

In each attack the squid surfaced astern of the *Brunswick*, which was steaming at 12 knots, and rapidly overhauled her, swimming backwards at about twice her speed. Having come up with her, the squid then swam on a parallel course some 50 yards distant until it was about 100 feet short of the ship's bows, when it made an abrupt turn inward at high speed and struck the hull "with a very determined thud" about 150 feet forward of the stern. It then extended its tentacles, which were as thick as "an 8- or 10-inch pipeline," and probed about with them to obtain a purchase, but, unable to obtain a grip on the smooth plates of the hull, the squid gradually slipped along and into the propellor, which chopped it to pieces.

Groenningsaeter's account of this fantastic experience makes it clear that all three squids surfaced with the deliberate intent of pursuing and attacking the *Brunswick*. And he suggests that since in each case the ship was struck at a point one-third of her length of 500 feet from the stern, the squids were striking at what they mistook for the series of low ridges known as humps that take the place of a dorsal fin on a sperm whale.

As to the question of whether the sperm whale controls the numbers of giant squids, the implications of Groenningsaeter's account are that *Architeuthis* is sometimes the attacker and the sperm whale the prey. And the largest squids, whose devilish beaks measure 9 inches in diameter, must prove formidable opponents even for bull sperm whales, which average 50 feet in length and weigh 40 or 50 tons. The largest architeuthid captured weighed 2 tons and measured either 52 or 55 feet, of which the cylindrical mantle, 12 feet in circumference, accounted for 17 or 20 feet and the arms, as thick as a man's body, 35 feet. Its eyes measured 7 inches by 9 inches. However, on the evidence of the scars left by the suckers of squids on the surprisingly thin hides of sperm whales, which are not much thicker than a sheet of carbon paper and very susceptible to abrasions, there are much larger architeuthids than this inhabiting the ocean. A squid's suckers include bony rings with teeth, and, as a rough-and-ready rule of thumb, the diameter of the suckers is about one-hundredth the length of the mantle. Four-inch scars, attributed to the suckers of squids with mantles about 30 feet long and with 50-foot tentacles, are quite often borne by harpooned sperm whales. What, then, must have been the monstrous size of that architeuthid which branded one whale with a sucker scar verified as 18 inches in diameter, even if a reduction of an inch or two is made to allow for the tremendous underwater suction pressures? In his massive inquiry into the fact and fiction concerning sea serpents, Bernard Heuvelmanns indicated that squids with overall lengths of 150 feet and weights of 50 tons are not the delusions of superstitious sailors and fishermen. Better still, a by all accounts reliable amateur naturalist, J. D. Starkey, who spent seven years of his life at sea, has published in the zoological magazine *Animals* an entirely convincing account of an architeuthid which he saw from a British Admiralty trawler when anchored one hot night off an atoll of the Maldives in the Indian Ocean. There was no moon that night, but Starkey had hung a cluster of light-bulbs low over the glassy water at the trawler's stern, intending to do some fishing with hand lines. At 2 A.M., while he was watching the wonderful variety of marine life attracted to the lights, all the fish suddenly vanished.

The water appeared to become opaque as the bulk of something filled my view. As I gazed, fascinated, a circle of green light glowed in my area of illumination. This green unwinking orb I gradually realised was an eye. The surface of the water undulated with some strange disturbance. Gradually I realised that I was gazing at almost point-blank range at a huge squid. I took my torch . . . walked forward . . . and shone the torch downwards. There, in the pool of light, were its tentacles . . . these were at least twenty-four inches thick. . . . I walked aft, keeping the squid in view. This was not difficult, as it was lying alongside the ship, quite still except for a pulsing movement. As I approached the stern, where my bulb cluster was hanging, there was the body. . . .

Gradually the truth dawned, I had walked the length of the ship, 175 *feet plus*. Here at the stern was the head or body, and at the bows the tentacles were plainly visible. . . .

The giant lay, all its arms stretched alongside, gazing up, first with one eye, then with both eyes, as it gently rolled. After fifteen minutes it seemed to swell as its valva opened fully and, without any visible effort, it "zoomed" into the night.

Groenningsaeter, in describing the squid's attack on the *Brunswick*, noted that it left behind a strip of black water during its run up, and its speed was so great that this inky water trailed behind like an elongation of the squid. In the choppy sea it was difficult to distinguish between the two; and he added that if he had been standing on a sailing ship's low deck, instead of on the motor vessel's lofty and also steady bridge, he might easily have mistaken the squids for sea serpents. No doubt many sightings of sea serpents and other marine monsters have in fact been those of giant squids, just as many others have undoubtedly been of oarfish, which reach lengths of more than 20 feet and sometimes swim on the surface of the sea, when they resemble snakes or eels with long dorsal fins. The rays of an oarfish's fin, placed just behind its head, are elongated and bright red and could be responsible for the frequent reports of a sea serpent with a head like a horse and a flaming red mane. In this connection Cousteau records witnessing several ribbonfish (relatives of the oarfish) swimming up the long cable of an underwater camera dangling from the *Calypso*. These were 6 feet long, though only an inch thick, and were "seemingly constructed of silver foil overlaid with a few orange and vibrant blue patterns, and with their flat foreheads sprouting orange antennae."

Heuvelmanns considers that three-fifths of nearly six hundred reported sightings of unknown sea beasts he has examined must be treated as reliable descriptions of animals unknown to science, which can be assigned to seven separate categories ranging from tropical saurians through gigantic "eels" to long-necked "serpents." However, only one sea serpent has ever been captured, and this was the $62\frac{1}{2}$-inch long larva of an eel, which was netted in 1930 at a depth of about 900 feet to the west of the Agulhas Bank, between St. Helena and the Cape of Good Hope. If the ratio in size of this larva to the adult of the species is similar to that of the larva to the adult of the common European eel, then it was destined to grow into an eel 90 feet long. But we do not know, of course, whether the ratio is similar; the adult may be no larger than the larva.

With regard to the possibility of one type of sea serpent

being a gigantic eel, Heuvelmanns quoted from the logbook of the barque *Pauline*, commanded by Captain George Drevar. On July 8, 1875, the *Pauline* was twenty miles off Cape São Roque:

> The weather was fine and clear, wind and sea moderate. Observed some black spots on the water, and a whitish pillar, about thirty feet high above them. At the first glance I took all to be breakers as the sea was splashing up fountain-like about them, and the pillar a pinnacle of rock, bleached with the sun; but the pinnacle fell with a splash, and a similar one rose. They rose and fell alternately in quick succession, and good glasses showed me it was a monstrous sea-serpent coiled twice round a large sperm-whale. The head and tail parts, each about thirty feet long, were acting as levers, twisting itself and victim round with great velocity. They sank out of sight about every two minutes, coming to the surface still revolving; and the struggle of the whale and two other whales, that were near, frantic with excitement, made the sea in their vicinity like a boiling cauldron; and a loud and confused noise was distinctly heard. This strange occurrence lasted some fifteen minutes, and finished with the tail portion of the whale being elevated straight in the air, then waving backwards and forwards, and lashing the water furiously in the last death struggle, when the body disappeared from our view, going down head foremost. . . . Allowing for two coils round the whale, I think the serpent was about 160 or 170 feet long, and 7 or 8 feet in girth. It was in colour much like a conger-eel; and the head, from the mouth being always open, appeared the largest part of the body.

Five days later, when some eighty miles east of São Roque, the same "eel," or one similar to it, was again sighted by the *Pauline* "throwing its head and about forty feet of its body in a horizontal position out of water as it passed onwards by the stern of our vessel."

We still know nothing about the life histories of these various kinds of "sea serpents." On the whole this is surprising, because the immense bulk of most of them suggests that they are more likely to inhabit the twilight zone than the abyss; though if some are a kind of eel, then they are likely to be bottom-dwellers and not to float to the surface when dead and are therefore never washed ashore. But sooner or later an adult "serpent" of one form or another will be captured or cast up on a beach and examined by a zoologist before decay sets in.

8: The Drifters

More than 85 per cent of some fifteen thousand known marine species of fish inhabit the relatively shallow waters over the reefs and banks of the continental shelves, with optimum conditions of food and shelter. The enormous quantities of fish landed by the world's fisheries are virtually all caught on the banks, and the greater the distance from these, the less the numbers of fish in the twilight zone, though not perhaps in the deeps. But this does not mean that the surface layers of the rest of the ocean are inhabited by relatively few fish; their incidence in these unfished millions of square miles has been greatly underestimated because of the absence of shipping and because of the almost total lack of research into the life of the upper waters. Almost every oceanographic expedition has concentrated mainly on trawling and dredging for planktonic life in the deeps and for the benthic or bottom fauna and the sediments of the abyss. Could not some enterprising expedition equip rafts for exploration of the ocean's upper waters? The *Kon Tiki's* 4,000-mile passage from Peru to Polynesia took ninety-seven days, during which period not a single ship was sighted, but the crew was never without company. Dorados (dolphin fish) were about the raft every day of the voyage in schools of up to thirty or forty, the same dorados and also pilot fish accompanying the raft day after day. Hardly a day passed without flying fish, some no more than an inch or two long, landing on the raft. There were porpoises in schools whose length and breadth appeared endless, sharks constantly, and whale sharks rubbing their monstrous backs against the bottoms of the great balsa logs. When in the Humboldt Current in particular, the crew often wondered if the whole of this vast ocean current was not full of fish. Their silent raft was just another fish in the sea, with no noisy engines to frighten other fish away long before the crew could sight them.

There is indeed life everywhere in the ocean. Shoals of sea snakes 3 or 4 feet long are encountered in mid-Pacific. All, with one exception which swims ashore to lay its eggs, are exclusively marine and indeed virtually helpless ashore because they are not equipped with the terrestrial snake's large flat belly scales. In calm weather they feed among the plankton or catch fish while lying almost motionless on the surface; and they have been encountered in fantastic aggregations, forming strips 60 miles long though only 10 feet wide when, presumably, engaged in gargantuan mating carnivals.

"Once when we were out on the open ocean," wrote Hans Hass, "We met another boat dancing happily along the waves. It was the shell of a cuttle-fish. . . . A crab sat on it as captain, and small barnacles were attached to it as crew. They too were outsiders sailing off for a life in a new realm."

Small crabs, some no larger than a fingernail, abandoned a bird's feather on which they were sailing in favor of the *Kon Tiki*; for the molted feathers of boobies and albatrosses have their part to play in the ocean's ecology. Some flying fish anchor their eggs to them and so does the ocean's only insect, *Halobates*. A variegated blue and black on the upper side and terra-cotta beneath, the uniquely pelagic *Halobates*

Halobates

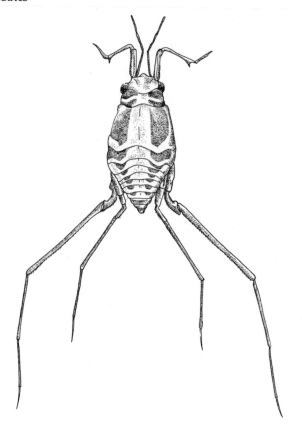

is a relative of the pond-skater, a kind of water-strider, and can skate delicately upon the surface of the sea; it is known as the Jesus bug. Supported only by the surface tension of the water, each of its six feet rests in a minute depression as the insect rows itself along at amazing speed with its middle pair of "oars," which are feathered with a line of very fine but stiff hairs. The stern pair is employed mainly for steering, the bow pair for support. Beebe describes how two clusters of electric lights focused upon a 20-foot circle of a Cocos Islands tide-rip attracted a hundred *Halobates*, which etched the sea's surface with a maze of shooting lines. And in the inshore waters of the Galápagos they were in solid sheets of thousands—all immature. Of all the ocean's mysteries, none is more perplexing than the survival of the *Halobates*. A single booby's feather, floating in mid-ocean, may hold twenty thousand of their eggs, deposited by perhaps a thousand females. The unlikely suggestion has been advanced that feathers entrap fresh water in the form of raindrops, essential to the development of the larvae. But if the insects' backs are wetted they become waterlogged and sink. How, then, do they survive tropical downpours? Where do they find shelter during storms? On what do they feed—on diatoms? On small insects, such as midges, that have fallen into the sea?

All the flotsam and jetsam of the ocean—drifting tree trunks, boxes, light-bulbs—quickly become the encrusted homes of small oceanic animals. But the most extraordinary of these microscopic island havens on the shelterless plains of the ocean are blobs of fuel oil, which become populated not only with barnacles and hydroids and egg-laying *Halobates* but, most remarkably, with a small fish which almost exactly resembles the oil blob in both shape and color. Since

fuel oil has been floating on the oceans of the world for only
about forty-five years, this fish cannot have evolved this
resemblance in so short a period. Presumably it previously
resembled particles of wood or bark or weed, though none of
these can be said to resemble a blob of oil closely. All that
one can say is that this "oil-fish" may have selected its new
home shrewdly, for a predator that had previously encountered oil might be wary of attacking any object simulating
it.

Pieces of drifting weed provide the majority of the ocean's
island havens. In this instance too, almost all their most
active inhabitants, whether prey or predator, resemble the
weed in color and may be further camouflaged with stripes
or bars, as if their ancestors had been domiciled in this unique
ocean shade for a million years. One must presume that this
camouflage was originally developed either among coastal
weedbeds or in oceanic concentrations of weed, such as those
of the Sargasso Sea, which must have come from the former.
Probably the initial deposits of the several million tons of
weed in the Sargasso were various brown algae which
hurricanes wrenched from the rocks of Florida and the West
Indies and which then drifted in the currents of the North
Atlantic and the Gulf Stream into this anticyclonic vortex of
calm. There, in this area of little rain or wind, high evapora-
tion and very clear saline water, the weed accumulated,
because more flowed in than flowed out. This process may
still be continuing, but the bulk of the weed must now be
indigenous, because the amount flowing in could not maintain the existing area which it covers. The individual plants
in these floating fields probably propagate from broken-off
branches, which bear spherical pea-sized floats that keep
the flat leaflike blades on the surface in the sunlight.

The Sargasso is not that dreaded mythical ocean swamp in which ships were doomed to eternal stagnation. When Beebe's *Arcturus* passed through it in 1925 he observed that it consisted of numberless patches of weed, seldom larger than a man's head, and in calm and storm alike these averaged only one to every hundred yards. Ever curious, he went down to investigate the fish's viewpoint. It was as though he were floating beneath a dense grape arbor, with the sun shining through a mat of yellow-green leaves and the unripe fruit glowing like myriads of jade buds.

The antiquity of the Sargasso's indigenous population is confirmed by the remarkable resemblance of its inhabitants to their weed environment. The special adaptations of its fish, crabs, shrimps, worms and anemones can only have been evolved after millennia within it; and it is particularly inter-esting to find the minute pelagic anemones—russet, tawny, translucent gray with thread of bluish-violet across their mouths—traveling as freely up and down the fronds as their molluscan neighbors.

The sargassum fish has carried the art of camouflage to its ultimate refinement. Not only is the shape of its mottled body disrupted by markings that continue right across the iris of its eye, which is normally a very conspicuous object, but it is also blotched with white patches resembling the encrustations of the bryozoans—minute feathery marine animals—that frequent the weed and have bizarre outgrowths of skin that mimic the structure of the weed fronds, over which it clambers with the aid of its pectoral fins, though, being a predator, it can also swim fast. Beebe noted the extreme reluctance of any of the Sargasso's inhabitants to leave the shelter of the weed. They are indeed entirely dependent on it and have developed special organs of attachment both for themselves and for their eggs, so that they will not suffer the terrible disaster of sinking into the abyss below, down, down, down for almost four miles—not that any would survive to reach the bottom. By swimming around and around, the flying fish bind the weed with silklike threads of nylon strength into solid balls, to each of which they affix hundreds of eggs, for these, being heavier than water, would sink if not attached to some floating object. The fry, when they hatch, will be brown, the color of the weed. Only when they mature and leave its shelter will they become the blue of the open sea.

We know, thanks to years of shrewd detective work by the Danish scientist Johannes Schmidt, that all European and American eels are apparently born in the deeps of the Sargasso Sea, but its surface waters may hold the answer to another of the many still-unresolved mysteries of the ocean. Although there are five species of sea turtles, all of which lay their eggs on sandy beaches, no one has ever seen the young ones for the first year or so after they have hatched and scurried down to the sea. However, since young green turtles hatched in captivity eat sargassum weed, sleep supported on rafts of it, and search among it for the small soft-bodied animals on which they feed, the inimitable Archie Carr, who has devoted more years than any other man to field research on turtles, suggests that the young of some species may pass the first months of their lives in the virtually unexplored Sargasso.

Although turtles are mainly inhabitants of coastal waters, they may also be met in the open ocean in widely dispersed schools of fifty or a hundred, each turtle several thousand yards from its nearest neighbour. Floating idly on the surface with a third of their carapaces awash, they serve as convenient resting platforms for wandering boobies and even penguins. The *Kon Tiki's* crew observed one turtle being attacked by a dozen dorados 400 miles south of the Galápagos Islands, and three more when 500 miles equidistant from the Galápagos and Easter Island. Marine turtles do not paddle in the manner of fresh-water turtles, but employ their flippers as wings, literally "flying" through the water at speeds of up to 20 knots. They could therefore travel a considerable distance in twenty-four hours. But numbers of turtles are involuntary travelers in such great ocean currents as the Gulf Stream, that vast planetary swirl, as Carr has described it, spawned in the Gulf of Mexico from the waters forced through the Yucatán Channel by the equatorial current and the easterly trade winds. From the pile-up of water in the Gulf, a level 18 inches above the Atlantic, springs the head that drives the sun-heated water clockwise around the eastern arc of the Gulf and nozzles it out through the Straits of Florida. From the union of this Florida current and the Antilles current the Gulf Stream emerges to begin its 3,000-mile drift across the Atlantic to northwestern Europe, towing with it leathery turtles, from the Caribbean to Norway (for it is unlikely that these are wanderers from a colony in the Mediterranean), and groups of loggerhead turtles to southwest Britain during the period between August and February. One of the latter, stranded on a Cornish beach, was thoughtful enough to carry with it proof of its identity in the form of a tuft of American algae. However, most of the loggerheads reaching Britain may arrive on a main tributary of the Gulf Stream by way of the Azores, in the region of which considerable numbers of American turtles apparently make their landfall. On a day in early September, for example, when some 250 to 300 miles out from the Azores, the

It is difficult to determine whether the large jellyfish are single animals or societies of individuals concerned, respectively, with propulsion, protection, fishing, feeding and reproduction. Perhaps, as Sir Alister Hardy pondered, they are of some higher individuality beyond our comprehension. On the one hand, the individual polyps that hang from the undersurface of the float perform separate, distinct duties. On the other hand, their separate activities are clearly coordinated. One polyp, for example, acts as fisherman to provide food for another polyp whose mouth can be enormously extended. Each fishing polyp is equipped with a very long elastic tentacle serving as a fishing line, which, when fully extended,

Velella, *the by-the-wind-sailor*

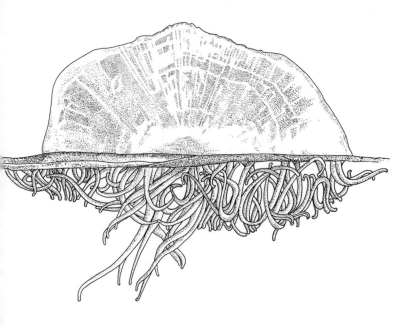

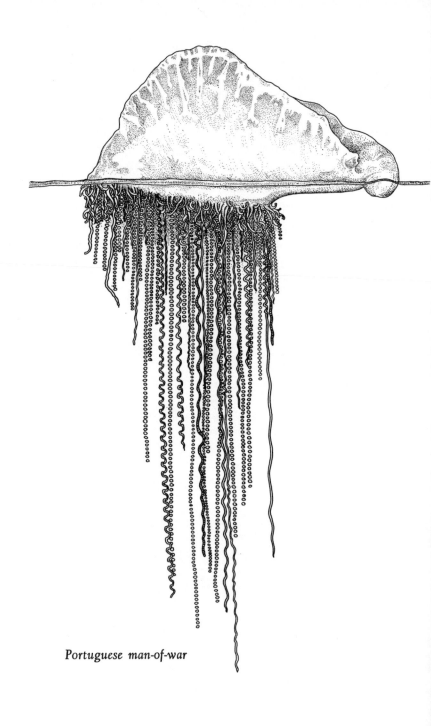

Portuguese man-of-war

reaches a length of as much as 30 feet—and, in the case of *Cyanea*, the lion's-mane or sluthers of northern and Arctic seas, up to 200 feet. The *Cyanea* can travel 600 yards in an hour by drawing in and expelling water with rhythmical expansions and contractions of its immense red "bell" 6 feet to 8 feet in diameter. The tentacles are heavily charged with stinging cells or nematocysts powerful enough to stun a fish as large as a mackerel. Since the man-of-war's tentacles are deep blue, they are probably invisible to fish, and when a fish blunders into the tentacles there is no escape, because it is harpooned, as Hardy expressed it, by barbed threads discharged by the thousands of nematocysts, and, at the same time, paralyzed by poison injected by the threads, which are hollow and act as hypodermic needles. When a fish has been harpooned the tentacles contract from their full length to only a few inches in a period of seconds, and haul up the struggling victim to the waiting mouthpolyps, each of which distends to cover a square inch or two of the fish's body. The fishing polyps then relax their hold, and the victim is entirely enclosed by, and hangs limply in, the bag of a composite stomach formed by the feeding-polyps, whose combined digestive juices slowly prepare it for communal absorption.

Inevitably, nature has found a way to take advantage of the possibilities of protection offered by the jellyfish's portieres of nematocysts, and to squeeze a few more animals into ecological niches.

Francis D. Ommanney has described how when the fry of cod, and also of haddock and whiting, have grown an inch or two, they seek out the lion's-manes, which in the spring abound in immense shoals in shallow waters, in order to obtain protection (and also shade on bright days) within their portieres:

When the water is clear, the great bells can be seen pulsing along like disembodied hearts, trailing their long tentacles, each surrounded by a cloud of little fish which dart back under cover of the bell at the least disturbance. It is a mystery how the fish themselves avoid falling victims to the stinging tentacles. They live in their floating home for a week or two and then settle on the bottom where they remain for the rest of their lives.

The fry of yellow-tailed amberjacks and harvest fish the size of a dollar make similar use of the man-of-war's sinuous tangle of thongs. When full-grown, however, they forgo this protection. But the men-of-war also afford shelter to an adult fish, the little *Nomeus gronovii*, which is rarely, or never, observed away from their company. *Nomeus* enjoys the additional protective advantage of perfect camouflage, inasmuch as its silvery-gray sides are striped with bands of the same deep blue as the man-of-war's tentacles. The few observations that have been made on *Nomeus* have tended only to deepen the mystery of the relationship between jellyfish and the various fish to which they afford shelter. Clearly, the swimming movements of the latter must involve inconceivably swift reflexes in order that they may avoid contact with the tentacles. But accidents have been reported in the confinement of an aquarium. In such cases the fish either died as soon as it was stung, or survived. Yet *Nomeus* has been observed vigorously attacking a man-of-war and nibbling at its tentacles, without suffering any ill effects, and *Physalia* tissues have been identified in the stomachs of *Nomeus*. *Cyanea*'s "guests" can safely remove particles adhering to its tentacles. The inch-long deep-blue tufted sea slug *Glaucus*, which passes its life clinging to the underside of the sea's surface film while floating upside down, not only preys upon the blue and gold jellyfish *Porpita* (a close relative of *Physalia*), but is able by some unimaginable mechanism to absorb *Porpita*'s nematocysts, undischarged and potent, into its own body, transfer them from its stomach to the filaments on its back, and employ them in its own defense.

Symbiosis also exists between small fish (and sea slugs) and the gigantic anemones of the Great Barrier Reef and other reefs in the Pacific and Indian Oceans. Unlike *Nomeus*, however, these anemone fish are not camouflaged. On the contrary, they display the most magically brilliant hues, inviting predators to pursue them and burn their snouts on, or be instantly killed by, the nematocysts on the anemones' spreading tentacles. But they themselves swim unharmed among the anemones, feeding on leftovers from their food, including scraps attached to the tentacles, while the anemones in their turn feed on any remains of the prey which the fish have caught outside the portieres and which, significantly, they have brought back to their retreat. Although a single anemone may provide shelter for ten fish, each species of fish adopts only one kind of anemone and in an aquarium will not approach the wrong host. It has been proved experimentally that the slimy mucus on the skins of these fish prohibits the anemones from discharging their lethal stinging cells; but do not other species, for which contact with the nematocysts is fatal, also secrete mucus? Robert Cushman Murphy was surely nearer the solution to this problem when, more than fifty years ago, he suggested that it was not actual contact with the nematocysts that triggered off the discharge, but some acid or other reagent in the skin of the victim, whereas symbionts such as *Nomeus* lack this chemical stimulus and can therefore shelter safely within the tentacles.

So far as the symbionts are concerned, the advantages in protection from predators evidently outweigh whatever disadvantages there may be, since they continue to lodge with their hosts. And protection appears to be the primary purpose of the relationship. In the waters off Haiti, Beebe observed as many as three hundred fry clustering beneath the bell of one jellyfish, and he also describes seeing half a dozen pilot fish sheltering from the same number of tuna under a large pink sea squirt shaped like a dunce's cap, known as *Pyrosoma*—another of those colonial "individuals," the largest of which is 3 or 4 feet in length. So long as the pilot fish remained under the cap, the tuna ignored them, though they were fully visible through its transparency, but when the pilot fish, disturbed by the ship, dashed out, all were snapped up.

One would suppose jellyfish to be entirely inedible and therefore of no interest to any predator. But, on the contrary, wandering albatrosses habitually feed on the man-of-war, and both hawksbill and loggerhead turtles devour the floats, wisely closing their eyes while brushing through the curtains of stinging tentacles. Jellyfish, including the minute *Velella* (another multiple individual, though product of a single egg), are apparently a staple food of the giant sunfish, which nibbles and sucks around the edge of the bell, demolishing it in from two to five revolutions, before moving on to another victim—though it is difficult to imagine what satisfaction a portly sunfish, weighing several hundred pounds, can obtain from this addition to its planktonic diet of a food composed of 96 per cent water.

The man-of-war fleets are also accompanied by a most ferocious, if unlikely predator, *Ianthina janthina*, the purple sea snail, which preys upon any animal it can contact, includ-

Sea anemone

ing its own kind. Though *Velella* is its most frequent victim, the man-of-war is also attacked, and two snails have been observed to devour the greater part of one with a 4-inch float in less than a day. To what do these snails owe their immunity from the man-of-war's nematocysts? Like squids and octopuses they emit dense smokescreens—in their case, a purple dye—when disturbed. But they also do this when chewing at a man-of-war's tentacle with the curved teeth in their mouth-slits. Does some constituent of this dye neutralize the nematocysts' poison? And how, for that matter, since they have no eyes, do these snails locate jellyfish? The solution to this latter problem is perhaps to be found in the observation that if any object approaches a purple sea snail from above it withdraws into its shell. It is possible, therefore, that its two forked tentacles are sensitive to gradations of light or possibly to vibrations, and that prey may be detected by them; although it could also be argued that jellyfish travel in such immense fleets that chance would bring the snails into contact with their tentacles often enough.

Evolution ran riot in the ocean. The incredible end-products of nature's ingenuity and the bizarre forms they took are innumerable, but the purple sea snail must be one of the most prized exhibits. We cannot be too grateful to a number of biologists who have assembled the jigsaw of this pteropod's life history. One is not surprised, perhaps, to learn that this extraordinary creature is hermaphroditic, even self-fertilizing, nor that it periodically ejects masses of actively swimming though minute larvae, with shells less than 1/300 of an inch in diameter, able to feed immediately on the plankton of the surface waters until they are large enough to build their own rafts and prey upon jellyfish. On the other hand, its four co-species attach egg capsules to the undersides of their floats—300 capsules to a float, 7,500 eggs to a capsule.

Consider also *Janthina*'s method of transportation. Other sea snails cling orthodoxly to floating objects and therefore have no control over their movements. But *Janthina* fashions a raft of bubbles, from which it hangs upside down with proboscis and tentacles inclined toward the surface. By extending the cupped forepart, or propodium, of its fleshy foot along the surface, the snail traps a bubble of air in the cup, coats it with mucus, and after from ten to twenty seconds' work presses it into place among other bubbles. Although the snail's shell is no thicker than paper, its occupant may measure more than an inch in diameter and must therefore be supported by a raft several inches long if it is not to sink into the deeps. Should the snail become detached from its raft, or the latter lose its buoyancy, the snail cannot rise to the surface again because it cannot fashion a fresh set of bubbles without access to air. It is equally doomed if it is cast ashore, because it cannot crawl back to the sea again.

9: Hosts, Symbionts and Cleaners

There is an element of symbiosis between the drifting fleets of jellyfish and the little fish dependent upon them for shelter, as the latter perhaps earn their keep by driving plankton within the jellyfish's portieres and attracting other fish to within reach of their tentacles.

A different type of traveling association, with elements of both symbiosis and commensalism (a relationship which is to the benefit of one party without affecting the other) is that of remoras and sharks. There are ten species of remoras, the largest from 18 to 36 inches long; and though sharks are the most favored hosts, whales, porpoises, whale sharks, rays, sunfish, marlins, sailfish, tuna, swordfish, tarpons, barracudas and turtles are also exploited, while small remoras attach themselves to smaller fish. Nor are the possibilities of boats neglected, and Heyerdahl believed that some remoras accompanied the *Kon Tiki* throughout her crossing of the Pacific.

A remora is equipped with an adhesive sucker, in the form of a flat oval disk with a slightly elevated rim and eighteen transverse vanes, on the top of its head. By erecting the vanes a vacuum is created, and the suction fixes the remora to its host. The fact that those remoras which attach themselves to the backs of their hosts must necessarily travel upside down presents no problems. Since they are a uniform gray above and below, they are inconspicuous either way up, though when they are excited longitudinal bands of white spread along their entire bodies. The powerful nature of the suction is illustrated by the fact that native fishermen in many parts of the world—Cuba and the Caribbean, north Australian waters, the South China Sea and especially off East Africa— catch turtles with the aid of remoras.

The remora, attached by its disk to the bottom of the fishing boat, travels to the turtle grounds. There, a cord from 180 to 300 feet long is made fast to the remora's tail. And the remora either quits the boat voluntarily on sighting, or sensing by some other faculty, a turtle (or shark or large grouper for that matter), or it is thrown in the direction of the turtle. Once a remora has attached itself to the nape or back of a turtle, the latter can be played until exhausted, with the remora remaining clamped until the turtle is lifted out of the water. East African fishermen reckon that, nine times out of ten, three remoras are required to hold one turtle. James J. Parsons writes that in Australian, African and Caribbean waters alike, the turtling remora is treated as a domestic animal, stroked, spoken to with soft words of encouragement or thanks, and fed special food. And when it fails to perform, it is verbally scolded, whipped with a small stick, or even bitten on the tail.

There would appear to be three advantages to remoras in

their association with their hosts. The latter carry them to a succession of new hunting grounds for the small fish and crustaceans on which they feed; the concealing bulk of their hosts may enable them to get close to their small prey; and their hosts may also provide them directly with food, for remoras have been observed to release their hold on feeding sharks in order to shoot out and snap up scraps, and then return to attach themselves once again to their transporters. Some species perhaps make more use of transporters than others, for Hans Hass observed that during the daytime remoras in the Red Sea were very rarely attached to hosts—though this does not rule out the possibility that they were attached when resting at night. The remoras that teamed up with him when he was skin-diving swam under his belly or between his legs but made no attempt to latch on to him. Moreover, although large remoras were swimming beneath and close to the bellies of nearly every one of a school of manta rays, darting out from time to time to snap up small fish, they never attempted to attach themselves to the mantas. Instead they followed almost every move of the mantas with dexterous strokes of their tails and maintained their exact positions beside them. If a manta spun round in alarm, its attendant remoras also accelerated and, though left behind initially, soon overhauled it.

Pilot fish, though free-swimming, probably keep company with sharks and rays, and also boats, for the same reasons remoras do, and they display the same ability to maintain exact position with these companions. A thumbnail of a pilot fish, wriggling just ahead of a shark's snout and keeping its precise distance, is, suggests Cousteau, held there by a compressibility wave. The *Kon Tiki*'s crew caught a great many sharks. As soon as one was gaffed aboard, its attendant pilot fish, varying in size from 1 inch to 2 feet, would take up position alongside the raft's centerboards or just ahead of its bows. At one stage the raft was acting as host to as many as forty or fifty pilot fish, though some of these deserted her when a very large blue shark swept past in pursuit of a school of dorados.

The symbiotic association of one fish with another is probably much commoner than has been supposed, though the advantages of the association are not always apparent. Little skipjacks often follow barracudas or sting rays; dorados associate with white-tipped sharks in the Atlantic, and on one occasion in the Red Sea, Hass saw two of these sharks accompanied, one by a blue mackerel, the other by a yellow mackerel. Both were keeping close to the sharks' fins, responding with precision to their every movement, and possibly snapping up scraps of food. It seems surprising that sharks should tolerate the presence of fish large enough to make a meal. And it is still more surprising that in another instance a 13-foot shovelhead shark should allow a 20-pound pompano to nudge it vigorously and persistently with its head while swimming close behind its dorsal fin. Almost all basking sharks have lampreys attached to them. Leaping baskers are perhaps attempting to shake off these pests, which reach lengths of up to 3 feet and even 6 feet, according to Gavin Maxwell. Lampreys prey on large "soft-skinned" fish, sucking away their flesh with their radulas (fleshy funnels armed with horny "teeth") and conveying the flesh back to their mouths with powerful muscular and "toothed" tongues. Since a basking shark's hide is too tough to be pierced by a lamprey's radula, one presumes that lampreys, like remoras, take advantage of the sharks as transporters to carry them within easy range of shoals of fish feeding on plankton; just as, when homing to spawn on the stony bed of a river, one may hitch a ride on a salmon running upriver.

The large silvery wreckfish (a grouper) may also be an example of one fish making use of another as a stalking-horse. In warmer waters of the North Atlantic, wreckfish are very frequently to be found lurking under floating logs or oil drums, waiting to snap up the small fish that feed on barnacles. They also undertake remarkable vertical migrations, for they have been speared at depths of 100 feet and photographed from a bathysphere at 2,300 feet, and one swam up the long cable of Cousteau's *Calypso's* underwater camera. On another occasion, when the *Calypso* was working over a sea mount rising to within 600 feet of the surface in mid-Atlantic, several large mantas circled around her, and from the underwater observation chamber in her bows Cousteau discovered that every one of the mantas was accompanied by a medium-sized wreckfish swimming with it in perfect unison. Since the wreckfish had changed color to match the white of the mantas' bellies, he conjectured that they were able to take advantage of the concealment provided by the latter's immense "wings" to snap up those fish which, since mantas are plankton feeders, habitually approach them without fear.

However, the master exponent of hunting with a stalking-horse is the trumpet fish (or flutemouth) of reef waters. It is also a master of camouflage. It is checked with brown and gray and slender as a stalk of the bushy sea whip, the Gor-

Trumpet fish

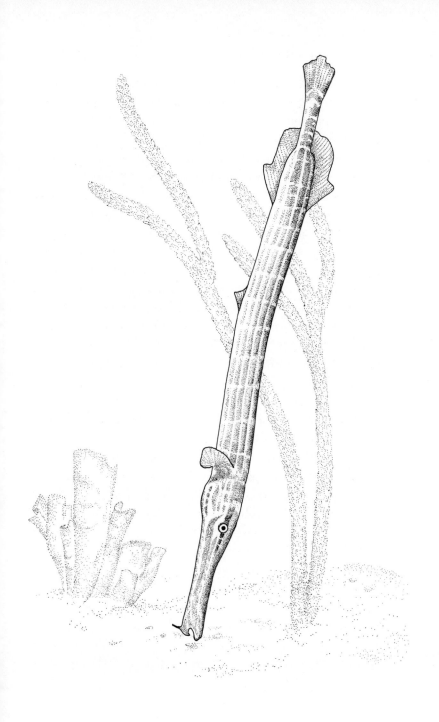

gonia coral. When alarmed, it takes advantage of this likeness by adopting a vertical posture and allowing the current to sway it in rhythm with the Gorgonia. Instead of the protrusible lips common to most fish, it has a fantastically long trumpet-shaped trunk. Its most often observed hunting technique is to hang stiffly, head downward, among the clumps of Gorgonia until a fish darts by too closely, when it strikes down with its trumpet and the fish vanishes into it. But sometimes—or perhaps more usually, who knows?—a trumpet fish will shoot up and lie along the back of a parrot fish, so closely aligned with it that it might be mistaken for the latter's dorsal fin. No matter how vigorously the parrot fish endeavors to shake it off by darting hither and thither, twisting and turning, the trumpet fish retains its precise alignment by some unimaginable tie. Now, parrot fish graze on coral polyps with their frontal teeth, which are fused at top and bottom into a kind of beak as sharp as a chisel, and crush the coral with powerful grinders set well back in their throats. Since parrot fish feed exclusively on these polyps, which are poisonous to other species of fish, the latter are not afraid to swim close to them. This affords easy prey for the trumpet fish on the parrot's back, though it is impossible to conceive how the trumpet fish learned to adopt this ruse. The parrot fish themselves, variously colored blue, red, green or black and white, are extremely conspicuous among the reefs. Because their poisonous diet renders them inedible, is one to assume that their extravagant colors advertise the fact that they are inedible or harmless? Or do parrot fish of one calor elicit aggressive reactions from those of another color, as Konrad Lorenz postulates, with the result that a school of parrot fish of one color maintains a measured distance from that of another color, thus ensuring that available supplies of coral polyps are evenly distributed among the variously colored parrot fish seeking the same food on the reefs?

And what do the transporters and stalking-horses gain from these associations? The answer would seem to be that in most cases their symbionts free them of some of the parasites with which all large marine mammals and fish are infected. There are no reefs or encrusted pilings on which to scratch oneself in the open ocean. Whales and great fish must be tormented by the irritation of sea lice and other parasites, for a whale may be the floating home of more than a hundred thousand lice. Even schools of rainbow runner fish, those 3-foot "cigars" of a fantastic blue with yellow stripes, will swim quickly up from astern of a shark and scrape themselves along the file-rough skin of its back. The frequent ocean-shaking leaping of great whales and rays, which crash back on the surface with a thunderous impact, is no doubt mainly impelled by the urge to rid themselves of these ectoparasites —though not in every case, for both manta rays and spotted eagle rays also leap in order to give birth in mid-air to their young which, as soon as they are ejected, spread their pectoral fins and make a parachute descent. Manta rays and whale sharks also habitually rub against boat bottoms in order to scrape off parasites, and are much feared by fishermen on this account, as they might capsize the boats. Since parasites tend to concentrate on the inner sides of the head fins of manta rays, the latter are also prone to scrape along the anchor chain of moored fishing smacks, and take both anchor and boat with them, being powerful enough to tow moderate-sized boats for several miles. In themselves, however, manta rays are as harmless as whale sharks. Indeed, Hans Hass and his companion Weidler rode on the back of one whale shark in the Red Sea. And Weidler not only polished

Manta rays

the rusty haft of his harpoon on the shark's rough hide, but smacked its snout with the flat of his hand, thereby inducing it to open its mouth and allow Hass to photograph the cavernous interior. Perhaps the shark which, according to Hawaiian legend, towed two shipwrecked men by its dorsal fin for several hours through the night to an island, was a whale-shark.

The tolerance of sharks and other great fish towards their attendant remoras and pilot fish is therefore based in part on the services the latter render as parasite-removers. When sharks are unable to repair to reefs where recognized cleaning stations are established by certain species of small fish, remoras take over this duty. Indeed they have been observed to drive away specialized cleaners approaching their particular sharks. The frequent identification of shark parasites in the stomachs of remoras confirms their role as cleaners and also indicates another source of food guaranteed by the association. The 9-inch remora that plucked at the nipples of a member of Hass's crew when he was diving over a reef in the shallow waters of a lagoon, perhaps, mistook them for parasites. Remoras have also been seen to enter the mouths and gill-covers of sunfish, probably in search of parasites. And according to Hass a school of a dozen pilot fish (zebra-striped with vertical dark-blue bands) will swim in fan formation in front of a whale shark's colossal jaws and swim in and out of the cavernous mouth, just as they will enter the mouth of a manta ray in order to clean the lower jaw's teeth, among which small crayfish lodge. Both sharks and rays permit these liberties, while the pilot fish, for their part, apparently recognize the vast mouths of rays as refuges and swim farther into them if alarmed.

Manta rays pay regular visits to reef cleaning stations, and Hass once watched eight rays circling around a Red Sea clump of coral 25 feet in diameter, while awaiting the attentions of several hundred mouth-cleaners. When they finally came to rest with gills wide open, 6 or 8 feet above the coral mound, battalions of cleaner-fish emerged to deal with them. Some examined the vast expanses of the rays' bellies, others wriggled into the narrow gills and in due course reappeared from the mouths.

Only when divers were able to rid themselves of their cumbersome helmets and enjoy relative freedom of movement beneath the sea was it realized how widespread is this cleaning symbiosis, which includes the removal not only of ecto-parasites but of dead and diseased tissue and those fungoidal growths and bacterial infections of the gills to which fish are particularly susceptible in tropical seas, where the majority of cleaner-species are found. The latter are specially equipped for their duties with such tools as pointed snouts and thin tweezer-like teeth, and also employ primitive forms of display and posture with which to advertise themselves to prospective clients. Six kinds of shrimps and more than forty species of fish, notably gobies, wrasse, damsel and butterfly fish, are now known to specialize as cleaners. And the young of many larger reef fish also act as temporary cleaners until they grow too big to be interested in parasites as a source of food. The cleaning instinct, or perhaps the immediate need for food in the form of parasites and tissues, is not so highly developed in some individuals or species as in others. And perhaps all cleaners have alternative sources of food. The small brown señorita wrasse of the Californian kelp beds removes parasitic copepods and isopods, minute crustaceans, from a variety of clients such as sunfish, bat rays, black sea bass, opal-eyes, blacksmiths and topsmelts. A señorita is frequently the focal point of a densely packed school of clients milling around it excitedly. But at another time a señorita swimming slowly by, with clients taking turns to position themselves directly in front of her, may ignore them and slip away to nibble casually at some floating minutiae. One large kelpfish was observed to solicit a señorita five times before the latter could be induced to remove a parasite that was annoying it.

Regular servicing stations are established near such salient sea marks as rocks, coral heads, wrecks or patches of white sand. One species of popular cleaner-shrimp uses an anemone as its headquarters. Though vividly patterned with white stripes and violet spots, the shrimp draws additional attention to itself by waving its grotesquely long antennae energetically and swaying its body to and fro whenever a fish swims by. If the latter requires attention, it stops a short distance away from the shrimp and presents the appropriate part of its body or mouth for the removal of parasites or of dead tissue around healed wounds. Cleaner-fish stations are also well advertised by their attendant—or attendants, for numbers may be working at one station. The slender finger-length neon gobies are, for example, distinguished by a brilliant electric-blue stripe with a black border. Since blue light penetrates the surface waters more powerfully than that of other wavelengths, this stripe illuminates them at a distance of several yards from the drab-green of their brain-coral stations.

However, individuals of such cleaner-species as the tiny yellow wrasse and cleaner-wrasse (which specialize in sharks) do not require their clients to visit regular stations, providing that they indicate by appropriate postures that they require servicing. Such postures include spreading the fins, raising the gill-covers, standing on the head or lying on the side, or floating upside down, inert, passive, as if in a trance. During one six-hour period of observation at a reef in the Bahamas some three hundred clients visited a cleaning station, and although some cleaner-shrimps paid the penalty of venturing into the mouths of the wrong species, such errors are rarely made by specialized cleaners because all potential clients indicate that they want service by the recognized postures. Even the fiercely predatory groupers allow cleaner-wrasse to enter their mouths, inviting them to do so by flicking their fins, and both wrasse and a red-and-white-banded shrimp are licensed to clean the teeth of the voracious moray eel.

Some clients employ color changes to single themselves out and perhaps invite preferential treatment. Thus one individual of a school of several dozen black-tipped fusiliers, floating motionless awaiting servicing, became very dark in color when a cleaner approached the school, and was the only member to be serviced. A predatory bar-jack swims more and more slowly as it approaches a neon goby's coral station, and its silvers and blues begin to deepen in color with the silver tarnishing and the blue stripes dulling and darkening until, when it ultimately comes to a halt, head down, over the coral, it is a uniform sooty-black. When satisfied that it has been adequately serviced, it gradually regains its normal coloring and becomes agitated, and should the cleaner persist in its attentions, it swims away. Such changes of color may perhaps serve to reveal any sores or blemishes more clearly. A coral cod's coloring of pink with blue spots, for example, changes to light gray with dark gray bands when it is being serviced.

The cleaner-wrasse, which advertise their calling blatantly by a broad black arrow that thickens along their silver and blue sides to the full width of the tail, and also by the peculiar looping undulations with which they swim, may actively solicit potential but unwilling clients. One swam boldly up to a large parrot fish with apparent intent to examine its gills, pectoral fins and thin lips, then dived unsuccessfully in pursuit of a blue surgeon fish with a brilliant yellow flag-tail, and finally darted after a large yellow butterfly fish passing through its servicing territory, overtook it under an outcrop of staghorn coral and cleaned it as it drifted placidly, head tilted.

After introducing this essential marine health service, nature has once again taken the opportunity to exploit the special features it incorporates. Certain small predatory fish, by mimicking the cleaners, are able to approach the latter's clients under false pretenses and take quick bites from their skin or fins. One of the blennies, for example, not only simulates the size, form and color of a bona fide cleaner, but even its advertising dance, in order to attack its clients. However, this dastardly impersonation apparently deceives only the younger and less experienced clients.

How important this health service is, and how considerable a part it must play in the lives of many fish, is illustrated by two facts. The first is that if all known cleaners are removed from a service station, not only do most of the normal clients disappear within a couple of weeks, but the condition of those that remain declines rapidly. The second is that oceanic fish, such as black sea bass and the giant sunfish, apparently undertake regular inshore migrations for the express purpose of being cleaned. Sunfish entering Monterey Bay have been seen to stop, flutter their dorsal and anal fins, tilt up their heads and pass into the semblance of a hypnotic trance. Schools of sea perch then raced up and, completely surrounding them, began a frantic cleaning of their massive grayish-white bodies, picking at their eyes, nostrils, mouths, gill-coverings and fins. On another occasion in the same locality, rainbow perch cleaned a number of sunfish of the small red "worms" with which they were infested.

10: Escape by Flight and Smokescreen

The eternal pursuit beneath the sea of prey by predator becomes visible to man when a glittering rain of projectiles shoots up from the waves. The flying fish are making their desperate escape from ravening bonitos or tuna, or from their most ruthless hunters, the dorados, which will themselves leap out of the sea with the impetus of their reputed 30- or 40-knot pursuit. Large dorados, $4\frac{1}{2}$ feet in length, hunt in pairs, and the small ones in schools. But all are intensely predatory, speeding instantly toward the slightest disturbance or splash in the water that might indicate a flying fish or small squid. Although they are reported to swim swiftly beneath the flying fish in order to snap them up when they ultimately drop into the sea, it would seem highly improbable that they could follow them by sight. Beebe observed that when a gar fish missed its strike at a flying fish, it became confused, made short rushes in various directions and failed to notice its prey when it came down again only 20 feet away. The ability of

156

flying fish to disappear out of the sea must confuse most predators.

There are a number of species of flying fish, measuring from 6 to 18 inches long: some with two "wings," the larger with four. Stroboscopic cameras, which repeat exposures at intervals of a fraction of a second, producing a picture of the successive positions of a moving object, reveal that a flying fish prepares for flight by folding its two enlarged pectoral fins (ribbed and flexible and placed high on the shoulders) against the sides of its cigar-shaped body, while swimming forward and upward at a speed of from 15 to 20 miles per hour. When its body is clear of the water and inclined at an angle of about fifteen degrees to the horizontal, the fish spreads its pectorals, though the pelvic fins remain closed, and sculls along the surface for half a second or a second by vibrating the tip of the lower lobe of its tail fin from side to side at a rate of up to fifty beats a second. When sufficient momentum has been gained, the pelvic fins are also spread, providing the necessary lift to raise the tail out of the water and make the fish airborne. With both pairs of wings fully spread, the fish is now gliding at the high initial speed of 40 miles per hour, 4 or 5 feet above the waves, and when taking off into the wind and striking an upcurrent of air it may rise high enough to land on a ship's deck 20 feet above the water. The larger the fish, the higher it can "fly," but it does so solely by gliding. Only one or possibly two species of fish, both freshwater, can fly by beating or flapping their pectoral fins. Nevertheless, as good a naturalist as Edward Wilson of the Antarctic noted in his diaries that he had twice distinctly observed (at distances of 10 to 20 yards) medium-sized flying fish flapping their wings like birds.

The oceanic flying fish's airspeed falls rapidly to 20 miles

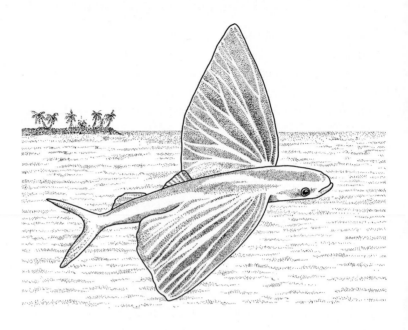

Flying fish

per hour during the 1 to 10 seconds of its glide, which may
follow a straight or curved course of from 20 to 200 yards, or
more than 300 yards in the case of large four-winged individuals. Beebe caught one of the latter 45 feet above the water.
But if the fish stalls, and also when it drops to the sea after
its initial flight, it can, by closing the pelvic fins, lower the
tip of its tail into the water, begin sculling again, and taxi
into another flight, which may be almost at right angles to
its original course. As many as eleven successive flights,
covering a distance of ¼ mile or more in 45 seconds, have
been observed. According to Cousteau, a flying fish, after

gliding over a long, straight course, can veer off into a cross-wind by manipulating its pectorals, or even double back downwind, misleading any predator as to its point of re-entry into the water.

Flying fish are not the only marine fish that can become airborne. The 18-inch pompanos of the Gulf of Mexico are reported to sail through the air on their sides with heads slightly elevated, while the flying fish's relatives, the elongated needlefish and halfbeaks, can break through the surface of the water at speeds of about 20 knots, and even shoot up vertically to a height of 16 feet. Normally, however, these inferior fliers proceed in 25-foot ricochets, dropping down again and again, tail first, to regain propulsion by sculling. Or they leap and skitter for 100 yards or more over the waves, with rigid bodies inclined at an angle of about thirty degrees and submerged tail lobes vibrating rapidly. They nevertheless travel with tremendous velocity, whizzing over the sea like silver spears. William B. Grey describes how, when he was collecting fish one night over a reef off Miami, his lamp disturbed a school of large houndfish (one of the needlefish), which began leaping in all directions; and as he was climbing into his skiff a 4½-foot specimen

. . . came sailing through the air in great leaps just at the edge of the light. Suddenly it changed course, and before I could move, it struck me like a spear. The snout went through my upper calf just under the knee and out the other side, then embedded itself in the wooden planking of the boat. For a moment or two I was pinned there, in such agony that I was hardly conscious, but then the fish tore itself loose and was off again.

More interesting aerodynamically than the flying fish is that versatile fish the flying gurnard, whose extremely thin and flexible, though enormous, scalloped pectoral fins include an upper winglike part that can be split at will from a lower part of several independently movable rays. By this device, which is comparable to the slotted wing designed to prevent stalling in the old Handley Page aircraft, a gurnard can not only embark on short gliding flights, but also use the pectorals as oars, or as fingers for turning over stones when it is probing for crustaceans and invertebrates. And the pectoral fins in conjunction with the pelvic fins enable it to walk slowly over the sea bottom. However, nature had introduced this slotted device much earlier in a pikelike fish that became extinct in the Cretaceous era (we presume). In this case a small pectoral fin was affixed to a greatly enlarged pelvic fin.

Fish are not the only inhabitants of the ocean that can "fly." When the sea seethes with hunting dorados, young squids work up a remarkable acceleration by pumping water through themselves, break through the surface at an angle, stern first, spread their broad tailfins and, with the membranes of their clustered arms providing additional support, can make 50- or 60-yard glides over the waves at considerable speeds. Witness a 1948 report by the research vessel *Pequena* that when she was slowed down by a 35- to 45-mile-per-hour wind, a "flying fish" (which in the event proved to be an 8-inch pale-green squid) shot out of the trough of a deep well 40 or 50 yards distant and, coming in at an angle at great speed, overtook her and landed on the fore welldeck. Unlike flying fish, squids usually fly in formation—though occasionally flying fish have been observed to do so. Oddly enough, the fact that squids could "fly" was apparently overlooked by most authorities for fifty years or more until Thor Heyerdahl logged them sailing over the *Kon Tiki* at heights of 4 or 5 feet, despite the fact that they have long been known to sailors as "flying squids." A re-examination of old records has brought to light a number of instances of squids of various sizes alighting on ships' decks, and even on their bridges some twenty feet or so above the water, during the hours of darkness.

No doubt both squids and flying fish take to flight mainly in order to escape from predators, though, as we have seen, both are attracted to lights at night. Gilbert Klingel, however, describes how, when his trawler passed through a school of small fish one night, some of the hundreds of squid that were preying on them were traveling at such speed that, when they neared the surface, they burst through and went skimming through the air for several yards before falling back into the sea or landing on the trawler's deck 6 feet above.

Marine animals feed on squids more than on any of the other cephalopods. The predators of squids include other squid, jellyfish, innumerable species of fish, especially dorados, and such birds as boobies, giant petrels, albatrosses and penguins. Wandering albatrosses feed almost exclusively on them. They are the main food of king penguins and make up a considerable proportion of that of emperors; the grounds of these birds' rookeries are littered with ejected squid beaks. The Falkland Islands sea lions eat so many that their intestines are often stained with squid ink. And elephant seals feed almost solely on squids, though it is difficult to understand how such colossal beasts can catch such swift and agile creatures. Squids are also preyed upon by all kinds of cetaceans, from dolphins to sperm whales. When Cousteau opened up a relatively small bottle-nosed whale an avalanche of undigested 3-pound squids poured forth, while in the recesses of its stomach were "thousands of their black beaks." Man himself accounts for a million tons of cephalopods every year, without observing any reduction in their multitudes. But evidence of overfishing is never apparent, or admitted to be apparent, until a species has been almost exterminated.

Young octopuses too are eaten by every predator, and large ones by sharks and whales. Merely to bring an octopus into contact with some kinds of starfish and brittle stars is sufficient to paralyze or kill it. The Indians of Puget Sound, south of Vancouver, who catch octopuses by sinking barrels into which the creatures can retreat when no rocky caverns are available, are aware of their antipathy to starfish and, in order to force the octopus to release its tenacious hold of its barrel, drop a starfish in. It must be supposed that the latter is able to inject some form of poison into an octopus; for when its normal molluscan prey is too large to engorge, the starfish extrudes its stomach through its mouth and between the mollusk's gaping valves, which it has slowly but inexorably pried apart with a 10-pound pull, and may inject it with poison in addition to digestive juices. Starfish evidently secrete some peculiar chemical, for even when one is at some distance mussels and oysters will close their shells, scallops swim away, and clams go jumping off on their "pogo sticks."

Although there are some free-ranging octopuses, the majority, rather than being swimming predators, are essentially inhabitants of the bottom, where they lie in wait in their lairs or half-buried in the sand for crabs, mollusks and fish. These they seize by a combined operation of their eight snaking arms, which spring from the head and are equipped with one or two rows of sucker-disks functioning as vacuum cups; or they envelop them with the webbed membranes that unite the arms at their bases and reach almost to the tips of the arms of some of the midwater octopuses. The prey

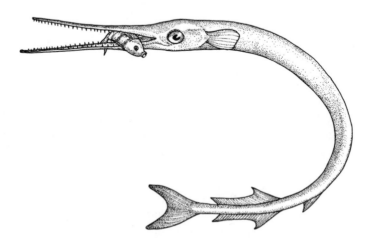

Needlefish about to eat a sergeant major

is then either killed with the sharp-pointed parrot-like beak of black chitin, or its central nervous system is paralyzed by an injection from the octopus's salivary glands.

In order to escape their host of predators the squids, octopuses and cuttlefish have evolved a number of highly sophisticated defenses. Only small squids can flee by shooting out of their pursuers' way. With the exceptions of the nautilus in its spiral shell and some free-ranging octopuses of the twilight zone, all cephalopods are equipped with a small ink sac, situated between the gills and terminating in a long neck connected to a funnel, through which the sac's thick fluid content can be discharged. As a generalization, one can say that a squid's ink is sepia-brown, an octopus's black, and a cuttlefish's blue-black. The latter's reservoir is the largest, and a small specimen, trapped in a tide pool 30 feet by 15 feet and 18 inches at its deepest, discharged sufficient fluid to turn the pool into a sea of ink in which it was invisible.

It has generally been supposed that the cloud of expelled ink serves the purpose of laying down a smokescreen between a cephalopod and its pursuers. And there is indeed some evidence that an octopus discharges its ink only when it knows that the avenue of escape on its side of the smokescreen is not blocked by a reef or other obstacle.

Gilbert Klingel was particularly interested in a large octopus that lived on Great Inagua's barrier reef. After a number of encounters with it, he described what happened when, wishing to test a theory that a light touch on its skin would leave a vivid impression of color, he stroked it along the side of its body with a stick. The stick was instantly snatched from his hand, to float to the surface, and the octopus flashed out of its fissure and ejected an immense cloud of purplish ink:

> For a brief moment I saw the octopus swimming away, long and sleek in shape, and then I was surrounded by haze. The fog was not opaque but imparted much the same quality of non-vision as thick smoke in dry air, except that I did not notice much in the way of wreaths. . . . From underneath the helmet there arose a faint odour quite unlike anything else. Fishy musk is the nearest description I can think of. The colour was most interesting, as I had always been under the

impression that cephalopod ink was black. Rather it appeared dark purple which later faded to a sombre shade of azure. . . . The ink spread out in a cloud extending over several yards; and in the still depths of the ravine took quite a time to dissipate. Actually it floated away as a hazy smudge before it evaporated.

The large *Gigas* squids of the Humboldt Current expel their ink under such pressure and in such volumes that the members of the 1940 Lerner expedition when hooking them with rod and line—though the strongest steel wire was often bitten through—were obliged to protect their heads and chests with pillowcases against the barrage of ink and water discharged over them and their boats. The immense quantities of ink discharged by these squids and also by the Inaguan octopus would certainly produce very dense smokescreens. But this is apparently not always, or not primarily, the *raison d'être*. When Otis Barton (the designer of Beebe's bathysphere) hooked up a *Gigas* with a gaff, and it discharged a cloud of ink as its normal reflex reaction to fear (or whatever may be a cephalopod's equivalent of that emotion), a slightly smaller squid immediately shot up from the depths through the cloud, cleared the surface, and attempted to seize the gaffed *Gigas*. Though falling short, it made two further attempts, passing through the cloud on each occasion. Similarly, Cousteau observed that the ink clouds emitted by octopuses in the Mediterranean were too small to conceal them from any predators and that fish swam freely through them. He did, however, note that a cloud, instead of dispersing, would hang in the water as a fairly firm block with a tail. And there is no doubt that in many instances it is the size and shape of the ink puff, which roughly resembles that of its owner, rather than any concealing properties it may have, that divert the predator's attack. A squid, for example, in order to escape from a predator, may change color, discharge its ink simulation, and then dart away while changing color again. In the meantime the ink has coagulated while sinking slowly, and may remain as a distinct shape for as long as ten minutes if not dispersed by the predator. Since squids usually associate in shoals, the effect of a number of them changing shapes and colors almost simultaneously would, one assumes, be most confusing to a predator, which would be as likely to attack the ink puff as it would a squid. Robert Schroeder, indeed, describes how, when swimming under water at night toward a pair of squids, he inadvertently shifted his head-light and suddenly realized that he was looking not at the squids but at "two spindle-shaped blobs of gooey brown ink." So closely did these resemble the squids that his eye had remained fixed on them while their owners darted away in the darkness. It was half a minute before he picked them up again, and in the meantime they had adopted a peculiar posture, designed perhaps to resemble a piece of floating weed, with their arms raised above their heads in the form of a lyre. Had it been daytime, the color of their arms would also have changed to the mottled greenish-brown of the weed.

A cephalopod's ink may include another protective device. Gilbert Klingel detected a faint musky odor in his octopus's cloud. Aquarium experiments indicate that the ink may affect a predator's sense of smell. A few drops deposited in the tank of a moray eel, that traditional predator on small cephalopods, incites the eel to swim violently around. But if an octopus in the same tank as eels expels a full charge of ink, the latter subsequently behave as if totally confused for periods of from one to two hours, and have actually nosed the octopus without betraying any signs of recognizing it as their habitual prey. Yet in normal circumstances their sense of smell is extremely acute. Cephalopod ink certainly contains some lethal ingredient, for a concentrated solution of it in a confined space, such as that of a bucket, results in the death of its owner in the short space of from three to five minutes.

Although the ink sac stores sufficient fluid to allow a number of emissions in quick succession, these may not always deter a predator. Though an octopus usually glides like a sheeted ghost over the sea floor or walks, spider-like, on its arms, it can also swim at a fair speed, either by inflating its head, or valva, with water and expelling jets of fluid, or by powerful contractions of its arm membranes. But its speed is not comparable to that of a squid, and a member of Cousteau's diving team, Dumas, had no difficulty in overtaking one. This octopus, having failed to check Dumas' pursuit by the discharge of several ink-bombs, was obliged to fall back upon its last line of defense. Plunging down, to freeze on the bottom, it changed color and pattern instantaneously to match those of the latter. A cephalopod's powers of camouflagic color-changing are superior to a chameleon's. In one-seventh of a second a small squid can flash from pure white to mottled green, and then to brick-red and back through green to white again. These abrupt and kaleidoscopic alterations in color no doubt cause a predator to hesitate, confused; but they also serve other purposes. Immense schools of squid hunt the 4- or 5-inch fry of herrings and mackerels just as the adults of the latter hunt young squids. Various species of squid employ different hunting techniques. Some shoot backward through a shoal of fish like miniature torpedoes, turning obliquely without perceptible change of speed to effect a capture, and killing their prey almost instantaneously by biting the back of the neck. Others zigzag slowly toward a fish until within striking range, when they shoot forward like arrows, with their eight arms spread "like the rays of a chrysanthemum" to grasp the fish harpooned by the long tentacles. However, should a dozen or more attacks prove abortive, a squid may settle on the bottom and simulate its color, waiting until an unsuspecting fish approaches, when it shoots up to make a successful kill.

Cuttlefish, the largest of which do not measure more than 5 feet overall, may employ a somewhat similar stratagem. By passing waves of color over the hinder parts only of their mantles, they perhaps divert the attention of their prey away from their arms, so that the tentacles (retracted in pockets beside the eyes when not in use) can be shot out inconspicuously at unwary prawns, shrimps and small fish. However, when hunting shrimps a cuttlefish may adopt the more positive technique of blowing random jets of water into the sand. Although these may not actually dislodge the shrimps, the latter reveal their presence when they move in order to throw more sand over their backs, which are uncovered by the jets.

11: Camouflage

Camouflage, in order to render oneself less conspicuous, whether prey or predator, is a feature of life in the ocean. One of the commonest forms of camouflage in the upper waters is to be colorless and glassily transparent like the amphipod *Cystosoma*, a small crustacean, which can only be detected as a crystal-clear blob among the colored masses of other organisms. *Xenolepidichthys*, a deep and laterally compressed fish like an angelfish, has evolved what must surely be the ultimate in deception by transparency. Its clearly visible silvery gut is positioned at right angles to the axis of its body, and a predator must receive the impression of two fish, one swimming horizontally and the other vertically—an impression heightened perhaps by the position of the eye, apparently situated in the forepart of the gut. But the majority of fish in the upper 1,500 feet employ counter-shading, with dark bluish backs, lighter silvery sides and pale white undersides. Herring, mackerel, bonitos and tuna are obvious examples. Viewed from above, their blue backs are inconspicuous against the deepening blue beneath the surface, and their silvery flanks automatically reflect the changing colors of the surrounding water. Viewed from below, the white bellies are difficult to see against the glare of light from above.

Conspicuous red or yellow fish are not found in the surface waters of the open ocean, and only one species of sea snake is banded with those warning colors so common on land. However, as Hans Hass has pointed out, few fish have a fixed color pattern that can be termed normal, because their coloring is automatically influenced by such environmental factors as the temperature of the water or the color and consistency of the sea floor, and also by their own physical and mental state—whether they are hungry or alarmed or asleep or receptive to the attentions of a cleaner. If a certain nerve is injured, a fish loses control over the pigment coloring the rear part of its body, and this section becomes permanently gray or black. A blind fish is unable to match its color to that of the sea bottom. The normally white or pale-rose goat-fish becomes bright red when excited, and a dying dorado loses all pigment control and dies like a sunset. Whenever a barbel grubs a morsel of food from the bottom, the three sharply defined black triangles on its silvery body fade out and are replaced by dark transverse stripes on a pink background. Similar stripes, presumably for concealment purposes in this case, appear on the body of a barracuda when it is resting among a grove of sea whips, but disappear when it becomes active. Camouflagic blue dots and transverse stripes appear and disappear on a sleeping tobacco-pipe fish (a relative of the trumpet fish) as it rocks to and fro in the rhythmic swell just above the bottom.

Beebe has described a night scene on the bottom of Inez Bay off Baja California. Rockfish were lying on their sides or leaning against rocks, deeply asleep. Groupers were resting flat on the sand, on an even keel or listing to port, but motionless, even when the beam from a suspended flashlight struck full upon them. Single puffers, with patterns of bright yellow circles and bands on their jet-black bodies, drifting slowly near the surface and apparently asleep on their fins, were also oblivious of the flashlight. In the shallows near the shore several hundred of these puffers were clustered close together on the sand—here five or six lying head to tail or side by side, there two or three lying across each other. In one place as many as sixty were in the beam of light at one time, sleeping right side up. Nearly all of them had thrown a thin coating of sand over their backs; but this in no way concealed them. Their conspicuousness suggested that they

Spotted goatfish

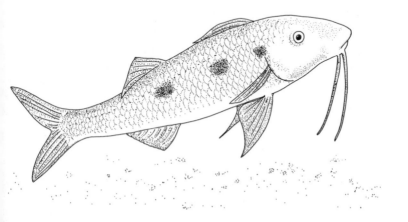

were not normally in danger of attack by night—as did the startled scattering in all directions and, bumping into weeds and rocks of twenty or thirty of them when a sting ray, frightened by Beebe, swam rapidly over them. Puffers can rest at night because they feed by day almost exclusively on mollusks and crabs, whose shells they crack with their upper and lower teeth, which, like those of parrot fish, are fused into a kind of beak. Rays and skates, on the other hand, have to feed by night. Southern puffers, no more than 7 or 8 inches long, are among the very few fish that cooperate in order to obtain their food. Although one puffer can bite through a crab's shell with its small beak, it cannot by its own efforts immobilize a large crab. This can be achieved only by a group of puffers working together.

Defensive measures by fish are not restricted to camouflage in one form or another. When a puffer or a porcupine fish, or even the 3-foot-long swell shark of Central American kelpbeds, is threatened or attacked, it rapidly inflates itself to as much as three times its normal size by gulping water and forcing it through its stomach into a distensible sac beneath. The porcupine fish (whose flesh is poisonous to man, if not to predatory fish) accentuates its unpalatability or fearsomeness by spreading all its fins. Then the waving white edges of the fins and the hard rays of the dorsal fin, armed with a venom gland, are very conspicuous even in deep water. Although the inflation renders the fish helpless, inasmuch as in this condition it can only bob about at the surface, belly uppermost, belching and bubbling as it deflates, the sudden dramatic increase in its size presumably prevents some predators from attacking it. And the additional barrier of the erected spines must make it too large to be swallowed by smaller predators. Indeed, it is said that if a porcupine fish is seized by a shark it inflates itself within the shark's jaws and, by impeding the flow of water through the gills, asphyxiates it. Nevertheless, even these extraordinary measures can be only partially effective, for porcupine fish, whether inflated or not, are heavily preyed upon.

Because nature is always playing one hand against the other in her efforts to maintain the ecological balance among the multitudinous variety of her fish, none of her defensive (or offensive) stratagems are 100-per-cent effective. Even the terrible tail spines of sting rays do not protect them against groupers, tiger sharks and hammerheads, in whose jaws and throats their spines have been found embedded, driven home by the muscles at the base of the whiplash tail. However, one cannot suppose that sting rays are extensively preyed upon by sharks and groupers; yet, if they are not defensive weapons, what is the true purpose of the saw-edged bayonets of bone, coated with enamel and with a groove down the side of each blade containing poisonous glandular tissue? A sting ray with a 10-foot "wing-span" may be equipped with as many as three of these spines, which are automatically replaced as they wear out, and whose mechanism is too complex not to have been evolved for some special purpose. Although one ray has been observed lashing another with its tail, the defense of territory or mate would hardly seem to warrant the development of such a terrible and complicated weapon. Nor could it normally be employed for killing prey, because the main food of sting rays is hard-shelled crustaceans and small agile fishes. In one night a Californian bat ray or eagle ray, having located a colony of clams by the jets of water they expel through their siphons, may dig a ditch 20 feet long, 12 inches deep and as wide as the spread of its pectoral fins, by flapping its "wings" and creating a current

that makes the sand and mud stream out behind it. Sifting the clams from the mud by this process, it spreads its wings over them and presses them firmly to the bottom, producing a suction vacuum, enabling it to prise them loose and crush them with the plates of its many rows of teeth, which overlap like tiles.

Electric rays pose a similar problem. On either side of the body beneath the "wings" there are immense numbers of vertical hexagonal columns, subdivided into smaller compartments containing electric plates with nerve-endings. These are capable of building up charges of more than 200 volts, powerful enough to knock down a man stepping on a ray buried in sandy shallows, but excessively powerful, one would have thought, for the size of any prey even a 6-foot ray might attack. But since a 30-inch ray will attack a 20-inch cod, it is possible that the discharge is employed to stun an overactive victim, as the shock is administered when the ray folds its head and wings over the latter. Its primary use is perhaps defensive, for angelfish, dogfish and conger eels have all been observed to shudder on coming into contact with an electric ray and retreat rapidly. And as electric rays live in murky waters, minute discharges of electrical impulses could also be employed for intercommunication as a form of sonar.

We have seen that, though pursued by innumerable predatory fish beneath the clear blue seas of the tropics and subtropics, and exposed to the attacks of such predatory birds as terns, noddies and frigate birds when they escape into

Porcupine fish

flight, flying fish are nevertheless highly successful, as their immense numbers and wide distribution indicate. No doubt their casualty lists are astronomical, but the numbers of those that die are of no interest to nature so long as sufficient live to guarantee the survival of the species. It has been estimated that off the Eastern Seaboard of the United States 1,000 million bluefish are decimating 10,000 million lesser fish, especially the 12- to 16-inch long oily menhaden, every summer day, harrying them inshore in such numbers that they pile up on the beaches in windrows; but the race of menhaden survives.

For that matter, inefficient species, or those unfitted to survive in a new environment, are permitted to succumb, as has happened often in the past, provided that there are other species ready to take their place. That nature abhors a vacuum is one of the few biological truisms that will stand up to the most searching examination, for the very good reason that if an environmental vacuum is established, then there is a danger of breaking a vital link in the endless ecological chain.

Because of the unusual nature of their escape technique, flying fish can travel singly or in small groups. In this they are exceptional. Most fish that are preyed upon travel in schools, and the school or shoal is the marine prey's commonest form of defense, especially in the open ocean, where any natural cover or concealment, other than that afforded by color camouflage, is lacking. Even reef-dwelling fish are said to form up into schools when migrating through unfamiliar water. If the ocean was originally populated from the shallow coastal waters, one surmises that these emigrants were obliged to form shoals in order to survive; and since they are composed exclusively of fish of the same size, though not necessarily of the same species, the inference is that a school originates in the coalescing of young fish of the same age in a spawning area, and that this initial aggregation subsequently attracts other similarly sized fish that swim at the same speed. Admittedly the losses among spawn and fry are astronomical, but if the estimate that one square mile of sea may contain the spawn of 500 million individual herrings is even approximately correct, then the basis is there for immense aggregations of young fish.

Once such a school has been formed it becomes almost as markedly a colonial individual as a jellyfish, with each fish placed as close beside or in front of or behind its neighbor as it can swim, without actually touching. Hence the prerequisite that every member of the school shall be of the same size and swim at the same speed. Any member's alteration in direction or speed is responded to instantaneously by the entire school. The human eye cannot detect any individual time-lag in the precision with which a school of fish executes an instantaneous maneuver. How can the fish swimming on the outer flanks of a school containing millions of individuals and extending over hundreds of square yards of sea apparently react at precisely the same instant as those in the center?

Hass has described his underwater experience of this phenomenon when he dived in among shoals of sardines that covered the sea for hundreds of meters around his ship and were so closely packed that when seen from above they appeared to form a single compact mass:

> So long as I kept quiet they hemmed me in on every side and I felt the movement of little bodies against my skin. If I moved, the living wall drew back as though at the wave of a magic wand. Individuals did not exist here; the entire shoal was one great super-individual, all the parts of which seemed to obey

one dominant will. Not a single member left the ranks when the whole body wheeled. The subtle sensitivity of the creatures' lateral-organs to oscillation kept them all linked to one another in a sort of electrical connection and every impulse became a spark that exercised a common control over all their movements. If I remained still, individuals reappeared and the shoal, with its hundreds of inquisitive eyes, advanced upon me.

As Hass has suggested, the answer to this problem of instant mass communication may lie in a fish's possession of certain unique sensory organs. The mechanisms of these, and how a fish makes full use of them, are complex and still imperfectly understood. And no two research workers come up with the same answers—nor, exasperatingly, do research workers always report accurately the details of their fellow researchers' experiments. However, it would appear correct to state that the most commonly possessed of these sensory organs is the lateral line, which is a series of fluid-filled pits along the fish's mid-body, and which usually branches into a network around the head. Successions of nervous impulses fired from hair-cells at the bases of the pits—intensified when one fish passes another—detect any vibration in the water, any change in the flow of the water along or projected against the fish's sides, any deflection of the bow wave in front of the fish's snout caused by an obstacle. The slightest current deflects the nerve hairs, which are arranged in such a manner that they trigger off different impulses, depending upon whether the motion of the water is toward or away from the fish. And their sensitivity is deadened only by random movements of molecules of water, which are themselves responsible for low-level "noise." Canals from the lateral line transmit the impulses to the central nervous system; and the latter must receive almost continuous sensations, with every vibration, every wave being meaningful and demanding a special response, if the individual is to survive. In this respect, Cousteau noted that pressure waves generated by a diver's rubber foot-fins would empty the immediate vicinity of fish, including those that were hidden behind rocks and unable to see the diver. The alarm would spread in successive explosions, the water trembling with urgency, and fish at a great distance would receive the silent warning.

Most fish can also sense any disturbance in the water, whether caused by solid objects or by the low-frequency vibrations of subaudible sounds, through receptors studding the skin in various parts of their bodies. Those of one of the deep-water gulpers, which has rather small eyes, are raised on stalks, as an additional aid, perhaps, to detecting its prey in the dark. And a rattail's large head is pitted with sensory canals. Thus a blind fish equipped with receptors is virtually unaffected by its disability.

The lateral-line receptors are reported to be sensitive to vibrations intermediate between those of very low frequency picked up by the skin receptors and those of relatively high frequency detected by the inner ear, which receives impulses from the lateral line or from the swim-bladder when underwater sound waves cause its inner walls to vibrate. Even aerial sound vibrations can be passed through water in sufficient strength to be detected by this hydrophonic apparatus. Hass noted, however, that a boat's loudspeaker music, reaching him under water without distortion, was ignored by various species of fish until finally a school of three hundred jacks approached and circled him and the microphone at a distance of 9 feet.

Fish may therefore be crudely said to "hear" with the whole body—but not with their ears, for the hearing organ (the cochlea) of all fish except sharks is minute. Their ears serve other purposes, since they house one or more semi-circular canals and a liquid-filled bladder. It is the latter, which is covered on the inside with the hairs of nerve-endings, that contains a number of the previously mentioned chalky growths or otoliths. At every movement of the fish these stonelike otoliths roll slowly from one hair to the next, and the resulting tremor is transmitted to the brain, enabling its owner to maintain balance and direction. Most species of fish, though responsive to low-frequency vibrations of up to 3,000 cycles per second, do not appear to respond to super-sonic sounds with frequencies higher than 8,000 cycles per second. But clearly such acutely sensitive mechanisms would enable every fish in the largest school, whether swimming in the center or on the flanks, to register instantaneously any alteration in the swimming motion of one or more of its fellows. It must be noted that herrings, which shoal in the largest aggregations, have no mid-body lateral line but a greatly developed system of canals in the head. Possibly this arrangement is associated with the fact that though herrings are equipped with gill-rakers, they do not secure their plankton at random by swimming with open mouths, but by aiming directly at individuals.

Although a shoal of fish presents a large target to a preda-tor and can suffer fearful casualties, its very numbers do constitute a form of protection, for when a predator dashes into a school, intent on striking at one particular individual, it must be confused in some degree when all the fish in the immediate vicinity dart off at tangents. But if the school can be forced to disintegrate, then the predator can snap up isolated individuals. To this end, predators often work together to herd a school in ever-decreasing circles and at the same time drive it up towards the surface, which, for all except specialist escapers such as flying fish and squids, presents an inpenetrable barrier that cannot be outflanked. Eventually individuals panic and dart out from the protective confines of the milling school, though they attempt instantly to slip back to its all-embracing protection. Those little tuna, the black skipjack, herd small schools of fish in this way, and three skipjacks have been observed following a school of mackerel shad at a little distance, with one skipjack at each rear corner of the school and the third behind them. If the school wheeled to one side, the skipjack on that flank would swim swiftly forward and herd it back on course again. And when one shad lagged behind the school it was snapped up by the third skipjack. Thresher sharks take more positive action when attacking a school, thrashing the water with their very long and powerful tails, which measure half of their overall length of 20 feet. There is no evidence as to whether this action panics individuals into breaking ranks, or whether it drives the school into a more easily attacked "mill," but these sharks are known to stun or disable fish with their tails. Even the simple rounding up of a school of fish is sufficient to lessen its protective value, as in an instance when several hundred porpoises (possibly dolphins, for these are usually referred to as porpoises in the United States), accompanied by between thirty and fifty sea lions and several thousand hovering gulls, made an onslaught on a 10-ton shoal of sardines. While the main body of the porpoises continually circled the shoal, a crescent-shaped line of half a dozen of them, side by side, repeatedly swept through it, with each of its members snapping up half a dozen or a dozen sardines at every foray.

Other species of predators may employ what might be

termed the psychological approach. Irenäus Eibl-Eibesfeldt, who accompanied Hans Hass on the *Xarifa* expedition, has described the reactions of a large school of silvery fusilier fish to the tactics of two big groupers. The fusiliers were feeding on plankton off a steep cliff in the Galápagos, with the groupers between them and the cliff. Almost imperceptibly the groupers closed on the school, until ultimately they were almost surrounded by the fusiliers. The latter kept their distance initially, maintaining a form of no man's land around the groupers. But as they gradually became accustomed to the presence of the groupers, they swam nearer to them. And in the end first one and then another fusilier would swim too close to the mouth of a grouper and be snapped up. Whenever this happened the equivalent of an electric shock, as Eibl-Eibesfeldt describes it, would pass through the school of fusiliers, and for a brief period thereafter they would swim in a more tightly knit shoal. But the effects of the shock soon wore off, and the process would be repeated. However, not every cautious approach by the groupers achieved a kill. They had to expend much time and patience over their hunting.

Other predators, of which barracudas are typical, hunt by the direct method of swift, slashing attacks. Sick or wounded fish may swim unsteadily or turn over on their sides, revealing silvery glints or causing abnormal vibrations in the sea. These will attract barracudas, just as any shining object such as a hook does, and they attack blindly, without pausing to reconnoiter. Similarly, if a diver jumps into the sea, sharks soon arrive and swim around inquisitively for a while; hence the occasional instance of a diver being attacked by a shark at the instant of splash-in.

The effect on fish of any abnormal incident is illustrated

by what happens when one is hooked or speared under water. Any predator in the vicinity immediately dashes toward the struggling victim—as one would expect; but what one would not expect is that there is a total reversal in the psychology of those that are normally preyed upon, for these also rush in. However, if the line slackens, permitting the hooked fish to swim normally, interest wanes and the previously excited participants swim away.

Normally barracudas do not attack human beings, though few divers feel at ease in the company of these sinister carnivores, which though averaging $2\frac{1}{2}$ feet in length, may grow to 8 feet and a weight of 100 pounds. But, like sharks, they are inquisitive, to the extent of swimming after people walking along the shore at the edge of the sea. All divers stress the prolonged and curious examination to which they are subjected by sharks. Dead fish, even though freshly killed, the barracudas ignore, because these do not make any sudden movements. A shark's olfactory organ informs it that a dead fish is edible.

It has often been asserted that fish do not sleep, but this is not the case. Even bottom sharks, which do not have to maintain the perpetual motion of their free-ranging relatives in order to breathe, can be seen sleeping among the coral in a sandy grotto, motionless except for the slow automatic widening and narrowing of their gills. Some parrot fish, breathing slowly and consuming only half their daytime level of oxygen, sleep so soundly that they can be touched or lifted without waking. One small West Indian species actually works for half an hour every night blowing a delicate bubble-like cocoon of mucus around itself, and works as long again at daylight to break out of this transparent envelope. Within its "bubble car" it can rest peacefully, immune perhaps from attack by such predators as moray eels, which smell out their prey. There is a monstrous green parrot fish, 3 feet or more in length, known to Cousteau as the "bumpfish" because of a bulging forehead, as hard as an anvil, which it employs to demolish coral, crashing head-on into a rock-hard block and smashing off chunks. These it grinds into particles with its powerful jaws in order to obtain the small animals that live in the coral. At night Cousteau observed that a school of bumpfish would split up into pairs or solitary individuals and go their own ways to sleep in recesses of the reefs. In their case, however, when one was touched on the tail it was galvanized into such explosive action that it rushed into a clump of coral weighing at least a ton and broke it clean off. At dawn the bumpfish would leave their retreats, rub themselves in the sand to remove parasites, and re-form into a school.

12: The Hunting Technique of Sharks

It has been said that among sharks only the mackerel sharks (the makos and the porbeagles) are equipped with the necessary speed and agility to kill healthy fish, and that other species prey upon wounded fish or scavenge. But this is of course not true. It is a fallacy based, no doubt, on the invariable presence of large numbers of sharks at the carcasses of harpooned whales and at whaling stations, together with their habit of following ships in order to scavenge on the garbage. Sharks regularly prey on tuna especially, and on squid, porpoises, seals and even turtles. Sir Arthur Grimble describes how every month on the days of the spring tides hundreds of tiger sharks would muster in the shallows off one of the Gilbert Islands in the western Pacific to harry those streaks of azure lightning, the 60-pound blue-backed trevally, which themselves were hunting the massed squadrons of 1-pound gray mullet. Puzzled by this monthly inshore appearance of the tiger sharks for a day or two only, Grimble set himself to unravel the mystery and discovered that when the high tides flooded through the channels leading from the ocean to a certain lagoon, they carried with them microscopic organisms that settled in the shallows. This manna from the ocean tempted millions of tiny soft crabs, none much bigger than a sequin, to venture an inch or two farther into the sea than they normally did. Waiting for the crabs in a couple of feet of water were millions of sardines, massed in silver clouds. Hence the mullet, the trevally, the sharks, and finally the Gilbert Islander with his ironwood shark-hook.

The truth is that sharks are remarkably agile, able to accelerate dramatically with a few flicks of their powerful tails and capable of overtaking warships traveling at 40 knots. That hunting sharks swim at high speeds is confirmed by the experiences of divers, who have noted that, though they might themselves have been swimming around for as long as half an hour without any signs of sharks in the vicinity, one or more would appear within a few seconds after a fish was speared.

After one twenty-four-hour storm the sea around the *Kon Tiki* was full of sharks, tuna and dorados apparently crazed with hunger and engaged in ceaseless strife and death-struggle—150-pound tuna leaped into the air with dorados in their jaws, and sharks slashed at the tuna. The frenzied nature of sharks' ravening attacks on harpooned whales and hooked individuals of their own kind might lead one to believe that they must consume large quantities of food at regular intervals or starve. But they can in fact store large reserves of food in their huge livers, whose weight may amount to a quarter of their total body weight; and captured specimens often refuse all food during the first six or eight weeks in an aquarium without suffering any disability.

Hunting sharks are equipped with three aids for locating their prey: sight, receptors to attract vibrations, and a sense of smell. Sight for them, as for all underwater predators, can be of significant use only at very close range, because of the restricted visibility which even in the clearest seas, such as those off the Australian Great Barrier Reef, is no more than 200 feet at a maximum. They are not, however, nearsighted, as has often been stated; for though they may not be able to distinguish the precise details of an object, they are quick to detect any movement both below and above water—as Cousteau discovered in one encounter, when, on the very instant that he saw a moderate-sized blue shark at the prevailing 75-foot limit of visibility, it immediately rushed toward him. And we now know that a number of species of sharks, if not all, possess cones associated with color vision in their retinas. Believing this to be the case, the commercial shark-hunter Captain W. E. Young, who killed a hundred thousand sharks in the course of a very long life, experimented when hunting in Australian waters with blue, green and white 8-inch nets 1,000 feet long and 16 feet deep, and found that sharks were invariably caught in the white section of a net. More important to a shark is the fact that it can perceive very slight gradations of light and make maximum use of the dim lighting in the twilight zone with the aid of a light-reflecting mirror (composed of large numbers of plates silvered with microscopic crystals of guanine) located behind the retina.

A shark's lateral-line receptors—its second aid to locating prey—can detect the vibrations of fish fin-beats at distances as great as 300 yards. The nature of these will convey to its nervous intelligence system whether they are those of a fish feeding, mating, alarmed or wounded, or of a shoal. In some instances a shark can probably orientate on its prey solely by guidance from its receptors, and its own sudden acceleration will be conveyed to the receptors of other sharks, and its significance understood. The Solomon Islanders, who eat sharks, have long known that they can be attracted by underwater sounds or vibrations, and they catch them by knocking coconut shells together on a pole under water. Possibly sharks can also detect the hydrodynamic sounds produced by water flowing over a fish's skin surface, and the swifter a shoal's movements, the louder the sound. However, experiments indicate that sharks are attracted not by continuous vibrations, but by those transmitted in irregular pulses and of a low frequency not exceeding 100 cycles per second (about two octaves above the bass end of a piano). Signals with higher frequencies have so far failed to attract them, although they are known to be able to detect those of 7,000 cycles per second or higher. Experiments off the coast of Florida with low-frequency vibrations simulating those set up by a struggling fish attracted several different species of sharks, which orientated direct from a distance of 300 yards to within visual range of, and then directly up to, the microphone. No fewer than 370 were attracted in this way, the first ones arriving from 11 to 54 seconds after the initial signal had been sent out. As their numbers increased, they began to exhibit that state of frenzy associated with their behavior at a slaughter of whales or other sharks.

A shark's third, and probably most important, hunting aid is its highly developed sense of smell, exercised by an olfactory organ consisting of two grooves on the underside of its snout; and two-thirds of its small brain capacity is concerned with this sense. The continual stream of water flowing over the sensitive surface of the olfactory grooves carries to them scents or odors of unimaginable delicacy. Gilbert Klingel has described how the shells of some immense razor fish crumbled to pieces while he was excavating them at a depth of 40 feet. The juices of the exposed flesh attracted a cloud of small fish and, in less than 4 minutes, a small hammerhead shark, despite the facts that there had been no previous indication of its presence within the 100-foot range of visibility and that there was only a slow current to disseminate the scent.

Experiments have indeed proved that a shark can detect chemical dilutions of a fraction of one part per million. If, for example, 500 milligrams of water are removed from a bucket in which a dozen small fish have been vigorously disturbed, and introduced into a tank containing sharks, the latter become very active within the space of a few seconds, circling around that part of the tank into which the infected water has been introduced. Other fish are also able to detect very weak chemical concentrations. Since some or perhaps all bony fish, when wounded or killed, emit a skin secretion, it is a reasonable assumption that this, when diffused into the sea, deters other fish of the same species from entering the danger zone. While this is primarily a communal protective device and is perhaps partly responsible for the temporary evacuation of fish from areas of underwater spearing, rather than their actual extermination, it must also have the disadvantage of attracting predators, such as sharks, equipped to receive these emissions. If a part of the skin of a dead fish is rubbed in water, and the solution poured among a school of fish of the same species, the school immediately swims away; and it may be this secretion that incites captive sharks when fish in the same tank, but partitioned off and invisible to them, are disturbed. The more frightened the fish, the stronger their "odor," and the more stimulated the sharks.

In addition to its main olfactory organ, a shark also possesses thousands of tiny sensory crypts on its skin, which act as taste buds; and also ampullae or cavities on its snout, which are probably sensitive to changes of pressure and possibly also of temperature. Once again, we are dealing with a subject that is very imperfectly understood. Various fish and marine mammals have taste-smell buds on their lips, cheeks, gills or chin-barbels, and even on their pectoral fins. A dolphin's tongue is studded around the edge with numerous papillae or small projections, which may be sense organs, for captive dolphins face an inflowing current of water with their mouths slightly open, as if tasting the water. They might therefore be able to pursue fish or other dolphins by "taste." Note also that marine mammals urinate at unusually frequent intervals, while sperm whales and belugas possess a gland in the anal region, secretions from which flow directly into the water. Although these secretions dissolve quickly, they may leave a taste trail.

If thus far we have been struggling mainly with problematical questions, at least there can be no doubt of the effect of blood on the carnivores, large and small, of the ocean. Hans Hass noted that he had only to open a mussel with a knife and produce drops of blood, for little fish to appear instantly. And Irenäus Eibl-Eibesfeldt describes how within sixty seconds of his wounding a fish and causing it to bleed only slightly, a slender white-tipped shark arrived on the scene and followed the exact trail of the fish to the wreck into which it had retreated.

A more detailed account of a shark tracking a wounded fish has been recorded by F. R. H. Jones. The victim in this case was a parrot fish, which had been wounded by a spear and had taken refuge in a coral head. A shark was attracted, and there was a chase among the coral, in which the parrot fish eluded the shark and swam away on a straight course for about thirty yards before making a ninety-degree turn and again pursuing a straight course. When the shark emerged from the coral a few seconds later, the parrot fish had already disappeared. Nevertheless, after casting around briefly, the shark swam off on the same course until, on overshooting the point of the ninety-degree turn, it slowed down, turned and, after another brief period of circling around, picked up the fish's change of course and followed it out of sight.

A shark, following a blood trail does so with head swinging from side to side, according to which of the olfactory grooves is registering the stronger scent, casting after its prey like a hound, in short turns and figure-eights. The olfactory grooves (and also the eyes) of that beautifully sinister monstrosity the hammerhead shark are situated on the terminals of the hammer-like lobes branching from its skull. They are there-fore widely separated and may enable it to hold to a scent trail more efficiently than other sharks. Certainly its numbers and wide distribution indicate that it is among the most successful of the genus, despite its handicap of being the only species not equipped with binocular vision.

Blood (unfortunately for an infinitesimal percentage of mankind) is the solution that attracts sharks most powerfully, though curiously enough they are strongly repelled by human sweat. A shark can detect one part of human blood in from 10 million to 100 million parts of water. And immediately it scents blood it is transformed from a cautious, even timid creature to a restlessly aggressive one. In this condition some species can be dangerous to man. Heyerdahl describes how normally, when the crew was sitting on the edge of the raft, any sharks in the vicinity would swim up to within 2 or 3 feet of their legs dangling in the water, but then turn quietly away. But if there was the slightest trace of blood in the sea, they would gather in numbers from a great distance, cleave like rockets toward the legs and dig their teeth into the log over which the feet had hung a moment before.

So too Irenäus Eibl-Eibesfeldt recalls an occasion when he and Hans Hass were surrounded by numbers of sharks, including twelve gray nurses and four black-tipped and some white-tipped. The larger sharks approached in ever-decreasing circles to within 6 feet, "examining us with cold and lively eyes which are strangely mobile and in sharp contrast to the rigid mask-like face. It was an uncanny experience being watched ceaselessly by those penetrating eyes." However, when the two men brandished their steel-tipped sticks, the sharks turned away. But when subsequently Eibl-Eibesfeldt harpooned a fish and placed its gashed corpse some 6 feet away on the edge of a reef, the snapping of some of the gray nurses and white-tips at the corpse and randomly at anything that moved, including themselves, became so potentially dangerous that the men were obliged to retreat.

When sharks are excited by the scent of blood, movements which had been previously disregarded, such as those of a diver's arms or fins, can provoke vigorous attacks. To deflect these, South Sea islanders, when swimming in shark-infested waters, take the precaution of unrolling a long cord as they swim out. However, 4-foot guard-sticks are normally effective defense weapons against all sharks except hammerheads and the great white shark (which, though widely distributed over all warm-temperate and tropical seas, is not very often encountered), provided that the diver is protected at the rear or from below when he is swimming upward. Swimming

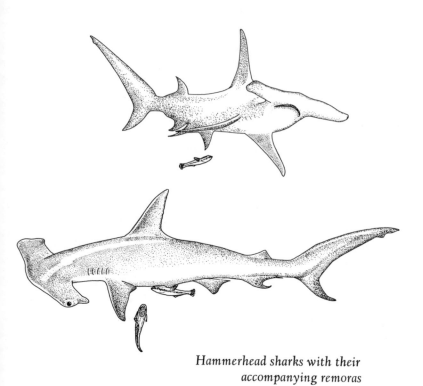

*Hammerhead sharks with their
accompanying remoras*

toward a menacing shark is also usually effective, because it is not the type of behavior to which sharks are accustomed, though a few have experienced the sensation of being hunted by sperm whales. Moreover a diver is a strange and therefore suspicious object, and it is perhaps relevant that when the normally iron-nerved Hass felt his body contract with terror on encountering a hammerhead, the latter's body also vibrated and shuddered, and the shark swirled around and shot off at such speed that the powerful strokes of its fins sounded like dull thuds. Swimming away from a shark, on the other hand, in an attempt to escape, is as likely to incite an attack as it is in the case of a terrestrial carnivore.

Bubbles floating up from an aqualung may act as a deterrent, and the vibrations set up by underwater shouting are also usually effective, since a shark is the only fish that possesses a mammal's type of ear. Hass, however, found that the noncarnivorous whale shark ignored his shouting and only turned slightly away when a force of 150 atmospheres of oxygen from his flask was driven against its head. A nonpredatory colossus with an armored hide and no known enemies, automatically sweeping up plankton and small game, is in no need of delicate senses. But shouting cannot be taken for granted as a 100-per-cent repellent against carnivorous sharks, inasmuch as those frequenting waters in which dynamite has been used to kill fish are unaffected and, since they probably associate noise with food, may indeed be attracted.

There are said to be one and a half million skin-divers, the majority of whom are spear-fishers, in the United States alone. And now that the sea is becoming the underwater playground and hunting territory of unprecedented numbers of human beings, it is important to know the answer to the question, why do some sharks attack men sometimes? There are, in fact, only a few hundred documented cases of attack, and these have been virtually restricted to seas with surface temperatures above 70 degrees F within 40° of the equator. Half have occurred in Australian waters, especially off Queensland and the great bathing beaches of the southeast, and a further one-fifth in southeast African waters. But no common denominator of attack can be discerned. All we know is that where large numbers of people are swimming in warm seas frequented by sharks, attacks are likely to occur.

And attacks may also be expected by shipwrecked sailors, whether on rafts or swimming in the sea. If there is blood in the water, the danger of attacks is increased. Possibly some older sharks may become habitual man-eaters after their first taste of human flesh. Possibly those sharks that normally prey on such mammals as seals are more likely to attack men. Some sharks that hunt in recognized territories may perhaps attack in defense of these, and the ever-increasing popularity of underwater fishing in many parts of the world could well result in an increase in the incidence of attacks on divers trespassing in such territories.

Ring-fences of polythene nets can provide some protection to bathers. Although it is true that a shark caught by the gills in one of these nets suffocates, because to breathe it must be able to swim forward and pass water over the gills, the very presence of a fence apparently and inexplicably inhibits sharks from attacking bathers, for no attack has ever been made by those sharks that have swum around the ends of fences into bathing waters. However, no adequate protection is available to the shipwrecked sailor, for despite a shark's sensitivity to the "smell" of blood and the secretions of fish, no chemical repellent has proved effective. Though copper acetate will repel some sharks from baited lines for periods of from three to four hours, Hass and Eibl-Eibesfeldt found this chemical as ineffective as others, whether they carried it on their bodies or stuffed it into a dead fish which a shark actually engorged. And Cousteau and Dumas were threatened by three sharks, which swam through a cloud of acetate in order to get at them.

There are some 250 species of sharks—depending upon what classification is accepted. So incomplete is our knowledge of sharks and, for that matter, of many other fish, that it is often impossible to determine to what particular species an observer is referring, even if he is employing the current nomenclature, which is subject to constant and exasperating revision, rendering identification more instead of less difficult. While it is of no consolation to shipwrecked sailors, it is a fact that fewer than a dozen species are regarded as sporadically dangerous by experienced divers. The remainder may or may not be as harmless as basking sharks and whale sharks, for it must be admitted that we know nothing at all about the habits of most of them.

The recognized potentially dangerous species are the great white shark in particular, the gray nurse (a sand shark), the mako, the black-tipped shark, the bull shark (alias the whaler, requiem or Zambesi shark), the tiger shark and the hammerhead, while juvenile Galápagos sharks have also proved to be extremely aggressive. The gray nurse and the whaler are particularly feared in both Australian and South African waters, and Hans Hass found that neither species evinced any fear of him, pushing their snouts close to his body. Cousteau, though threatened by gray nurses, was never resolutely attacked by any species; and tiger sharks, sand sharks and makos were all put to flight by various members of his diving crews. Nevertheless, his final verdict is that "it is impossible to guess how a shark will react; the more one sees of them, the less one knows them, and one mistrusts them more and more." Hass is still alive, despite skin-diving encounters with more than a thousand sharks, and despite the extraordinary liberties he has taken with them. Since he has suffered only one serious injury, inflicted in self-defense by a small brown shark only 5 feet long, which he had deliberately harpooned, the implications are that sharks are unlikely to press home underwater attacks on experienced divers prepared for their attacks and equipped with guard-sticks. Indeed, for a shark to attack a diver is probably exceptional. So far as I am aware there are, for example, no records of shark casualties among the large numbers of Japanese divers employed in collecting trepang (sea cucumbers) for the Chinese aphrodisiac market. But to bathers and shipwrecked sailors splashing about in the surface waters of warm seas, sharks are always a potential menace and are almost certain to attack if there is any blood in the water.

Little account appears to have been taken of the experiences of native fishermen in shark waters around the world. These would almost certainly throw a very different light both on the incidence of shark attacks and on the behavior of those species that are dangerous. Sir Arthur Grimble, for example, noted that though the Gilbert Islanders habitually killed the dangerous tiger sharks singlehanded with their knives, they greatly feared a slim shark exceeding 20 feet in length, known to them as the *rokea*—perhaps one of the blue sharks. The *rokea* normally hunted in deep waters but congregated in the 240-foot zone when the bonitos migrated inshore. And Grimble was himself a witness of an attack by one on a fishing canoe whose crew of two had hooked a bonito that was being pursued by the shark. The *rokea* stove in the canoe with three smashing blows of its tail and then swept one of the fishermen into the sea and butchered him. The other canoes then gave up trolling for the bonitos, for it was the islanders' experience that the *rokea*, having eaten human flesh, would attack the canoes unceasingly for the remainder of the day.

13: Underwater Sound, Sonar and Communications

Men in general have always believed the ocean deep to be an abyss not only of eternal night, but also of eternal silence. Yet Aristotle was aware, more than two thousand years ago, that some fish grunted and that dolphins squeaked under water and moaned in the air. So, too, Indian fishermen have long known that if one holds the handle of an oar to one's ear its blade, in the water, will transmit the "drumming" of sea perch. Ghanaian fishermen make similar use of a three-pronged paddle to detect the vibrations emanating from large shoals of fish and also from submarine reefs. The Arctic whalers of the nineteenth century were so familiar with the twittering, whistling, gurgling, chuckling, hooting, popping and puffing sounds emitted by herds of belugas that they named these white whales "sea canaries." But only within the past thirty years has it been fully appreciated how full of noises are the upper waters of the ocean. And only now are the crews of nuclear submarines lurking in deeper waters, discovering that their hydrophones are cluttered up with strange animal noises that they must learn to differentiate from those engineered by the instruments of other vessels searching for them above or below water. If there are any naturalists among those submariners, how they must bewail their misfortune that their monstrous coffins lack even a single scuttle through which they might peer at the unknown creatures that speak to them through the hydrophones.

Sound waves are transmitted under water with exceptional clarity and travel farther and five times faster than they do above water (at approximately 5,000 feet per second compared to 1,000 feet per second), and even quite small sounds carry great distances. A Weddell seal's trills and chirps, which have been likened to the tinkling of water in a cistern, have been picked up by hydrophones at a distance of 5 miles, while the explosion of a 6-pound TNT bomb can be detected more than 3,000 miles from its source.

Sonar (Sound Navigation And Ranging) was developed in the 1920s and subsequently improved upon by the British Asdic (Allied Submarine Detection Investigation Committee). Echo-sounder oscillators or transducers affixed to the hull rotated beneath the ship and were therefore able to search for shoals of fish up to 1,000 yards distant. In the early sonar the pulses from the transducers were transmitted vertically to the bottom and could return only vertical echoes. However, it was not until World War II that considerable interference on the hydrophone networks for submarine-detection on both the East and the West Coasts of the United States revealed that four kinds of vocal fish were producing widespread underwater sounds. And submarine commanders were quick to take advantage of these as camouflage for their own operational noises. This interference was caused by groans from both black and red drumfish, repeated bursts of drumming from croakers, and raucous honks from spotfish, hundreds of millions of which migrate into Chesapeake Bay in the spring.

Subsequent investigations have shown that there are numbers of vocal fish able to produce and control sounds for a variety of reasons. Howard E. Winn describes how the bright-red squirrelfish that live among coral reefs utter short grunts when defending their niches against others of their kind, and long staccato chatterings when approached by moray eels, even mobbing the latter with these calls. Vocalism is also associated with mating activities. In the late spring the males of the black drumfish and of the small singing midshipmen and other toadfish become aggressively territorial. In addition to repelling other males with series of aggressive grunts, the midshipmen produce a low, vibrant humming with their swim-bladders, while other toadfish "boop" intermittently like ships' sirens in order to attract females, accelerating their transmission when one approaches. Having secured mates, they continue to call until the latter's eggs are well developed. But the dominant vocal choruses are associated with dusk or dawn feeding. Throughout May and June in both Atlantic and Pacific waters the croakers, for example, maintain a daily underwater chorus that begins to crescendo about sunset, when they begin feeding, and rises steadily to a shrill uproar of harsh froggy croaks with a background of soft drumming. In Japanese waters, schools of a million croakers are reported to synchronize their drumming. The uproar continues at optimum level for from two to three hours, before finally declining after midnight to sporadic outbursts from individuals.

All sounds produced vocally by fish are resonant, guttural and low-pitched, with a hollow timbre similar to that obtained by knocking on a wooden wall with a hammer. Neverthe-less, the very low croaking of toadfish, which are bottom feeders, and the drumming of croakers spawning 50 feet below the surface are audible above water, and at close range under water their noise has been described as almost deafen-ing and has been variously compared to the sounds of nearby thunder, of a riveting machine, of a subway train, or of a pneumatic drill tearing up a pavement. Croakers have actu-ally registered 107 decibels, in comparison with the 80 decibels of a drill, though it is not clear whether or not this level was obtained through a hydrophone, which grossly amplifies underwater sounds.

All vocal fish are bony fish possessing swim-bladders. No sound has ever been recorded from a shark, whether in the sea or in an aquarium. Some fish, such as squirrelfish, thump with their fins against the part of their skin adjacent to the swim-bladder. Others—sea catfish, croakers, sea robins—drum rhythmically on the membranous sides of their swim-bladders by expanding and contracting strong muscles, and produce about twenty-four vibrations a second. The muscles could be compared to the strings of a guitar, with the bladder acting as a resonance chamber amplifying the snapping muscles, or, in the case of jacks, triggerfish and ocean sunfish, amplifying the sounds produced by rubbing together special teeth situated deep in their gullets. The swim-bladders of some fish are constructed in such a manner that when the fish expels a bubble of gas there is a mouselike squeak.

Hydrophones suspended in deep waters off Bermuda have picked up strange mewing sounds, shrieks and ghostly moans. And one used by the research ship *Atlantis* in the surface layers of the 17,000-foot deeps to the north of Puerto Rico picked up loud calls, followed at intervals of about 1½

Sea robins

seconds by fainter calls assumed to be their echo from the bottom. If this assumption is correct, the caller was swimming at a depth of about 11,500 feet. The structure of the swim-bladders in benthic or bottom fish and such abyssal species as the rattails does in fact indicate that they too must be able to produce sounds. These could serve as recognition signals in the darkness, and take the form of the modulated squawks, squeals and crackles of the sea robins, which, despite being bottom fish, are relatives of the flying gurnards.

Many fish also make nonvocal sounds, higher-pitched than those produced by the swim-bladder. Some, resembling the stridulation of crickets, result from the friction of one part of the skeleton against another part. Of a comparable nature is the squeaking made by spiny lobsters rubbing their antennae bases against serrated pads under their eyes. Since their anxious squeaking when they are approached rises to a shriek when an attempt is made to capture them, it presumably serves to scare away predators. There is also the clicking made by mating sea horses—superbly heraldic in purple, crimson, white or yellow—when tossing back their bony crests. And, most notable, the brush-fire crackling of *Crangons*, the snapping or pistol shrimps. Though *Crangon* is only an inch or two long, it is armed with one very large claw (half the length of its body) with a finger that snaps like the hammer on a gun. Lying close within the entrance of its burrow, with long antennae extended to detect any vibration in the water, *Crangon* waits until apprised of the approach of a small fish. Then, creeping out, it stuns the fish with its pistol finger and drags it into the burrow to share with its mate. The *Crangons* are forever clicking their fingers, especially when feeding at dawn and dusk, and their crackling is the dominant sound over rocky bottoms in warm, shallow seas within 35° north or south of the equator. It was an additional factor in the jamming of the United States hydrophonic networks, since when concerted it is reported to carry 2½ miles under water.

Another shrimp, inhabiting waters off the Florida Keys, also snaps a large red and white claw with the sound of a spring breaking under tension. But in this case the snap is to frighten away intruders, for the shrimp lives in association with a brown anemone. Any small fish that might nibble the anemone are repelled by the snapping claw, and it is known that the anemone may not survive for very long if its protector is removed.

A crackling similar to *Crangon's*, but of unknown origin, was picked up during Cousteau's deep dives in the Challenger Deep. While he was unable to trace the origins of this "remote creaking" sound, it is generally attributed to thousands of small shrimps scraping their pincers in concert.

Nonvocal sounds are made by fish when feeding. Bottom fish, such as flounders, rock cod, wrasse and rays, when grinding the hard shells of mollusks with teeth, make a filelike crackling noise, while triggerfish drill noisily through the shells with powerful chiseled teeth. Even herbivorous fish may make sounds when chewing up seaweed to which hard-shelled animalcules are attached. And these sounds perhaps attract other fish to sources of food, for when a selection of feeding noises is played back by a transducer to fish in an aquarium they may begin to behave as if feeding. But these, like vocal sounds, could also have the disadvantage of attracting predators. When, for example, the rasping feeding sound of an amberjack was played back, a barracuda immediately swam up to a point some 8 feet from the suspended transducer and faced it, motionless, for about three minutes. And a recording of a black grouper's low-frequency sounds attracted sharks from a great distance.

It was the anti-submarine networks that rediscovered, after twenty-three centuries, that marine mammals such as dolphins

also habitually employ a variety of underwater sounds, ranging from low-pitched clicks to high-pitched whistles. Skin-
divers, swimming under water among herds of porpoises,
have been able to hear the shrill pips of their mouselike
chirps and squeaks. Subsequently, intensive research in
oceanariums and laboratory tanks have proved that these
sounds are used not only for echo-location but also as a complex, meaningful and communicative language.

A dolphin is equipped with a variety of acute senses. When
at rest it is constantly transmitting, at intervals of 10 seconds
or so, trains of hundreds of exploratory shock waves in the
form of tiny clicks or bleep-bleeps at rates varying from 5 per
second to one every 20 seconds, which combine to form a
creaking or rasping sound. These are echoed back by any fish
or other object in the vicinity. And if the dolphin receives
such an echo, it transmits a different series of bleeps at the
rate of 100 per second, and increases the rate of transmission
as the fish draws nearer. Divers have described the fascination
of being approached by a dolphin employing the full range of
its sonar bleeps, with the pattern of the latter changing from
that of initial random exploratory search to that of definite
location and identification as soon as the intruder's presence
has been received on the dolphin's "screen," and before it
finally swims at high speed into the diver's field of view.
Kenneth Norris describes how the dolphin closes in on its
target with its head swinging in a more or less rotary motion,
sweeping its sonar beam back and forth across the target
area and saturating it with exploratory clicks until, finally, it
stops swinging and locks in on the target itself. If this is a
fish, it is approached directly and the clicks cease at the last
instant prior to its capture. So intense is the sonar beam that
a diver can actually feel the sound on his hands.

Dolphins both emit and respond to wavelength frequencies of from 100 to 170,000 cycles per second. Since low-frequency waves (recognizable as clicks or creaks to the human ear) spread throughout the sea without being deflected, these are most suitable for long-range detection up to distances exceeding half a mile, in the case of the dolphin. High-frequency waves (five or ten times higher than man can hear) return detailed information on close-range objects and also differentiate between a number of objects. The electronic sonar devised by man works on a single and unique frequency and can therefore receive only a single and unique type of information. But a dolphin's sonar can not only locate fish, but also distinguish between different sizes of fish by the differing patterns of their echoes. So sensitive is the dolphins' sonar that it enables them to detect single metallic threads only 1/5th millimeter in diameter (though not nylon threads, because these have approximately the same sound-frequency as water) and to evade every kind of net from the finest tulle to one with a 9-inch mesh. The echoes from larger meshes elude them, as these are too diffused.

A blindfolded dolphin, constantly broadcasting its trains of clicks, can unerringly negotiate mazes of vertical steel poles or distinguish between identically sized sheets of different kinds of metal, or differentiate eight times out of ten between steel spheres 2¼ and 2½ inches in diameter. But (and this is really brilliant) if a dolphin is asked to judge between spheres of identical size and type, it indicates that the problem is impossible by turning away from the apparatus, whereas it will continue to work at a solvable problem even if it has made errors. Nor are these the limits of a dolphin's sonic capabilities, for it can transmit *at one and the same time* to its calf or companions both clicks and whistles of different frequencies. Thus with a single burst of bleeps it can transmit or receive comprehensive information far exceeding that obtainable by man-made electronic sonar or by a single human sense.

Aristotle was also aware that though dolphins "have no visible ears they can hear sounds in water." Their hearing is indeed so acute that the slight sound caused by the dropping of a spoonful of water, or of a single pellet of buckshot, from a height of 6 feet into a tank is sufficient to trigger off a rapid transmission of location bleeps. But whereas the dolphin then orientates toward the shot, it ignores the spoonful of water, being able evidently to differentiate between the familiar sound of water and the unfamiliar sound of lead shot. Clearly, a dolphin must be equipped with an extraordinarily sensitive hearing apparatus. And an examination of its brain indicates that while it has little or no sense of smell, as we know it, and makes little use of touch, its optical nerve is relatively large and the aural nerve so large as to confirm a special development of this sense.

One of the bottle-nosed dolphin's most often heard vocalisms, when it is playing or cruising idly, is a high-pitched whistle produced by forcing air through the single blow-hole on the top of its head. A young dolphin is able to whistle immediately after birth and to recognize its mother's whistle. If the young is separated from its mother, it remains in one place, whistling loudly, until she returns. But this is not only a simple contact note employed to keep the members of the family or herd in touch, it is also emotionally expressive and communicative. A captive male whistled almost continuously for three days while swimming around the body of its dead mate. That he then died from the effects of a perforated ulcer is perhaps to be attributed to three days of starvation, perhaps not. All the members of a herd begin whistling if excited by a strange object. A wounded or sick dolphin repeats two particular and dissimilar very short, sharp high-pitched whistles—crescendo and decrescendo—over and over again. These distress calls silence all other dolphins in the vicinity and incite them to begin an immediate search for their companion. When it is found there is a complex exchange of whistling notes and the disabled dolphin is pushed to the surface and supported there by one or two members of the herd so it may breathe, in the same manner as a young dolphin (or a young sperm whale) that fails to swim to the surface within seconds of birth is pushed up by its mother. Moreover, the call sounds of one kind of dolphin are apparently meaningful to another kind, for when a trainer tried to remove a sick *Delphinus* (the common dolphin) from a tank shared by a false killer whale, also of the dolphin family, the dolphin began whistling. Whereupon the false killer whale "gently, but nevertheless very deliberately," pushed the dolphin out of the trainer's arms. When the dolphin was recaptured, the false killer whale grasped the man's leg, pressed it gently with its jaws and relinquished its hold only when the dolphin was released.

A dolphin's speaking repertoire also includes what have been variously described as whines, croaks, squawks and, when it is being fed in captivity, mewing and rasping sounds and loud and aggressive jaw-clappings. John C. Lilly, who has made the most intensive study of captive bottle-nosed dolphins, is in no doubt at all that, while some of these sounds are employed sonically, others form a complex speech. He goes further than this, believing that shrill modulated sounds are mimicries of human laughter and conversation, and that it may be possible to devise some means whereby men and dolphins can converse with each other. Cousteau makes the interesting point that while a dolphin's throat, tongue and lips are not adapted to pronouncing human words, there is in fact a whistling form of human speech with a considerable vocabulary in use in Mexico, the Pyrenees and the Canary Islands, which closely resembles the dolphins' whistles. Shepherds in the Canary Islands, for example, can converse on crags three miles apart in this whistling language. If you are conservative in your thinking you will no doubt agree with one marine biologist and his wife that "communication between men and porpoises, other than training commands, is pure nonsense." (So was space travel to an English astronomer royal.) If you are more adventurous, you will hopefully agree with Lilly. If, like myself, you have the misfortune to be an impartial skeptic, you will await further developments with an open mind and keen interest.

Whalers have long been aware that whales also exchange signals under water, and a hundred years or so ago a certain Captain Edmund Kelly out of New Bedford is reported to have developed a method of listening to their communications. There can no longer be any doubt that all cetaceans—the order of whales, dolphins and porpoises—are vocal, and there is little doubt that all have the ability to communicate with a more complex language than simple contact calls. Pilot whales, which commonly travel in herds of hundreds or thousands, are known to employ at least five different communicative sounds. And when the *Calypso* was in the Indian Ocean, 100 miles north of the equator, Cousteau listened to three sperm whales conversing with subdued and modulated sounds. Subsequently, when one of them collided with the ship, the injured whale gave mouselike squeaks, and then plaintive cries in reply to the piercing calls of its companions.

The two unhurt whales pressed their shoulders against it on either side and enabled it to raise its blow-hole above the surface. When Hans Hass was photographing underwater sperm whales being harpooned off the Azores, a dying female opened her lower jaw almost at right angles and uttered a deep, harsh, vibrating sound resembling the creaking of a huge barn door turning on rusty hinges. This death-cry carried clearly and powerfully beneath the sea. There is good evidence that a sperm whale can communicate its alarm or distress almost instantly over a distance of six or seven miles under water to other members of the herd.

The hearing of whales, like that of the dolphins, is remarkably acute. Whalers have always asserted that whales can hear the shouts of the lookout in the crow's-nest, and are particularly careful to approach sperm whales quietly. Although baleen whales have no external ears and the ear-holes, which are presumably closed under any considerable pressure of water, are so small that it is only just possible to insert a pencil into them, they possess, superimposed on the eardrum, a long waxy plug which acts as a sound-conductor. Incidentally, if this plug is cut longitudinally its annual growth layers are revealed, which, like those on the ear-stones of fish, might indicate a whale's approximate age. Research by this method has so far proved inconclusive, though an age of eighty years has been tentatively suggested for one examined fin whale. This is a most unexpected finding, for cetaceans mature so quickly that one would not expect them to live to the great ages traditionally ascribed to them. In the light of this suggestion, however, the Eskimos may be correct in maintaining that a whale's life span is of the same order as a man's; and we must perhaps give some credence to the assertion that "Old Tom," the physically unmistakable

leader of a pack of killer whales which frequented an Australian whaling station, was more than eighty years old when
he was finally washed up dead in 1928. But it must be
admitted that we know very little more about the life spans
of the various cetaceans than did Aristotle, who reported
that dolphins, marked by nicks on their tails, lived for
twenty-five or thirty years, a report which, if correct, indicates that they returned regularly to a home range. In our
own times there are apparently only the records of a male
sperm whale recovered with a marked hand-harpoon after a
lapse of thirty-two years and of a female after twenty-two
years; and that of the famous Pelorus Jack (or, more probably, Jill), a Risso's dolphin, who for a quarter of a century
—from 1888 to 1912—met and accompanied every ship
entering a certain six-mile stretch of water in Pelorus Sound,
in the dangerous seas between the North and South Islands
of New Zealand.

Since whales in general are responsive to a wide range of
sound-wave frequencies, there cannot be much doubt that
they are equipped with a sophisticated sonic system. Whalers
switch off their depth-finding apparatus when hunting sperm
whales, which are constantly to be heard clicking under
water. Baleen whales, which also emit squeaking sounds, are
so sensitive to asdic waves that they can be guided this way
and that by them. Without sonar, how could whales navigate
through the relatively shallow and murky North Sea? In
those waters no white light penetrates below 1,300 feet, and
only 1 per cent below 120 feet, while the maximum horizontal visibility may be only 56 feet—less than a medium-sized
whale's own length. Some whales frequent the still darker
waters below the polar ice, where even in the spring less
than 1 per cent of light passes through its 6- or 10-foot-thick

layer. How do the Weddell seals in the Antarctic locate their fish in almost total darkness hundreds of feet below the ice? Are they also equipped with sonar? During the last three months of 1964 Carleton Ray and William Schevill listened to Weddell seal "talk" through three hydrophones spaced at equal intervals on a 1,000-foot cable lowered through a hole in the 6-foot-thick ice of McMurdo Sound. When selections were played back on an underwater transmitter, replies were received almost immediately, and a puzzled seal swam up to look closely at the transmitter. At every repetition it returned for a further inspection, often mimicking the sounds being transmitted. A succession of visitors behaved similarly, and one, which was repeatedly attracted back by bursts of trans-mission, ultimately swam up through the cable hole into the laboratory hut in search of the invisible "seal." Confronted by two curious scientists, it withdrew after a decorous pause. Another visitor, which arrived within two minutes after the transmitter was switched on, although no seals had previously been visible, was aggressive, biting the transmitter and batting it with its fore-flippers. However, the transmissions were apparently not entirely convincing, for on the follow-ing day they excited comparatively little interest. Ray and Schevill obtained 400,000 feet of seal noises on magnetic tape and concluded tentatively that these were communicative and social rather than sonic.

The causes of the frequent mass strandings of such ceta-ceans as pilot whales, and less often of killer whales and false killers, and even of herds of sperm whales numbering as many as twenty or thirty individuals, have never been estab-lished. No doubt pilot whales often strand when attempting to escape from such predators as killer whales, and perhaps also when in pursuit of squids, which hunt fish in deep water

close in off Newfoundland coasts. Strandings of other cetaceans may be the result of a herd panicking when finding
itself in very shallow water or in the, to it, strange conditions of calm waters over sands and mudflats or heavy seas
breaking on rocky coasts. However, since the stomachs of
many cetaceans that have been examined have proved to
be empty or almost so, while the brains of other specimens
have contained parasites, their stranding may have been due
to physical or mental sickness. But, since we now conjecture
that whales make use of sonar, another possible cause presents itself. The majority of strandings take place on muddy
or gently shelving shores, from both of which sonic recep-
tion is of poor quality, with the echoes too reduced or too
confused to be understood by the whales. It could be argued
that this form of sonic breakdown is responsible for the
repeated observation that if only a part of a herd of pilot
whales strands, those afloat in deeper waters cannot be driven
away from their stranded companions. Although this
behavior could alternatively be attributed to the dominance
of the herd instinct, there are some very strange circumstances associated with it, for not only is the refusal to
accept freedom also characteristic of solitary individuals, but
if the latter or members of a herd are helped back into deeper
water, they refuse to take advantage of this assistance and
run themselves aground.

While stranded squids behave in a similar way, in their
case it seems that a squid in trouble will naturally employ its
most powerful means of propulsion in order to escape and jet
itself backward, thereby restranding itself. All cephalopods
have a highly developed nervous system. The nerve fibers of
large squids in particular are some fifty times thicker than
those of most other animals—.05 inch thick, compared, for

example, to man's .001 inch. The longer the nerve fibers the more rapid the conduction of any impulses to the farthest extremities of the squid's mantle. But although these giant nerve fibers furnish all cephalopods with extremely swift reflexes, and although there is no doubting the considerable intelligence of an octopus, which will squirt water with deliberate intent at a man if irritated by his experiments or by not being fed at the customary hour, one hesitates to assign similar "emotions" to an invertebrate cephalopod and a vertebrate whale.

Still, conservative zoologists, rather surprisingly and without embarrassment, refer to cetacean "suicides" for want of a more reasonable explanation. They cite the extraordinary case of a herd of some twenty pilot whales which, when first sighted through a telescope, were heading for the coast of California on a dead-straight course from a point about seven miles out to sea, and ultimately piled themselves up, without any apparent effort to turn aside, on the beach of a small cove. There was no question of this being an accidental stranding on a shelving beach, because deep water extended right up to the shore. Those who, with some reason, ridicule any connotations of "suicide" assert that all strandings are the result of a herd following its leader blindly. But why should the leader, if any, of these twenty pilot whales deliberately, from all accounts, run itself and its companions aground?

Anthony Alpers has said that the world of a cetacean is primarily an aural world and obviously not the visual world of man—though the human eye itself often merely amplifies the initial discoveries of nose or ears, especially among primitive peoples whose senses of hearing and particularly of smell have not been partly atrophied. To the extent that the world of, for example, a dolphin in the "silent" sea is in fact a noisy world of echo waves from shoals of fish and reefs and the sea bottom, this is true. And it may be that other dolphins and the fish it hunts are voices and vibrations rather than shapes, and that if a calf wants its mother, it listens rather than looks for her. Nevertheless, we know that some of a dolphin's impressions are probably received through sensory "taste" organs, and that, rather surprisingly, it has excellent vision both below and above water, despite the restricted range of visibility in the submarine world. It is very difficult to see through the surface of the sea from below at an angle of less than thirty degrees because of the sheen which is reflected downward. So the habit of dolphins and other cetaceans of leaping out of the sea may sometimes be for the purpose of obtaining an aerial view, just as killer whales may press themselves up over ice floes in order to look for such prey as seals and walruses.

Some species of whales, however, support themselves in the latter manner when blowing. In polar waters lesser rorquals, or red whales, frequently breach in narrow leads among the ice floes in order to blow, and Captain Scott described how on several occasions one of these whales rested its head upon a floe, with its nostrils just above the water-line: "Raising itself a few inches it would blow and then subside again for a few minutes to its original position, with its snout resting on the floe."

Captive dolphins frequently "stand" high out of the water in order to gaze around their tank and at spectators, and possess the extraordinary ability to stand literally on their tail flukes, with the remainder of their bodies out of the water, while at the same time backing 50 or 60 feet at a speed of 6 knots in order to catch fish thrown to them. Pilot

14: The Incredible Dolphin

The relationship of dolphins with man is more remarkable, and of greater antiquity, than that of any other animal. Neolithic man scratched the outlines of dolphins on the rock faces of his caves, and a gifted Cretan painter accurately portrayed *Delphinus* in the magnificent frieze in the Queen's Megaron in the palace of Knossos, which dates from around 2,000 B.C. Plutarch was aware of some special affinity between dolphins and men 2,500 years ago, for of *Delphinus* he wrote: "On the dolphin, alone among all others, Nature has bestowed this gift which the greatest philosophers long for: disinterested friendship. It has no need of any man, yet it is the friend of all men and has often given them great aid."

Traditionally, dolphins have always been the friends of fishermen and the rescuers of shipwrecked mariners. Herodotus recorded how the Greek musician and poet Arion, a contemporary of Aesop, was rescued by one in 600 B.C.; and

217

both Greeks and Romans (and also the Maoris) have cited many instances of dolphins saving men from drowning and of dolphins helping fishermen by driving fish into their nets. To this day the fishermen in the Rhone delta and in the Bay of Naples assert that dolphins deliberately help them in this way. So do the Moreton Bay fishermen of Queensland. And so, still more remarkably, do those in Brazil's Mato Grosso and those on the Irrawaddy in Burma, although the dolphins of those regions are freshwater species.

The shallow lagoons of the Rhone delta were inhabited by the dolphins' favorite fish, mullet. When the highest spring tides cut channels through the sandbanks to the lagoons, the mullet are able to migrate to the sea. Since the currents racing through the channels are too swift for fishermen to set their trap-nets across, they, reported the Romans, "called up" herds of dolphins, which stationed themselves at the mouths of the channels and drove the mullet back into nets set in the shallows. How the fishermen called the dolphins is not stated, though Pliny the Elder noted that "The Dolphin is a creature that carrieth a loving affection to musicke: delighted he is with harmonie in song, but especially with the sound of the water instrument, or such kind of pipes."

Is the "calling" of the dolphins folklore? Consider the testimony of Sir Arthur Grimble, whose integrity cannot be impugned. There were in the early years of this century hereditary porpoise(dolphin)-callers among the Gilbert Islanders, and Grimble was a witness of their incredible powers over, or affinity with, dolphins. On a dead-calm January afternoon he was met on the shores of the Kuma lagoon by the High Chief's hereditary porpoise-caller, who informed Sir Arthur that he would first have to go into his dream and dispatch his spirit to seek out the porpoises in their home under the western horizon and invite them to a dance, with feasting, in Kuma village. He thought that he would be able to call them to the lagoon by three or four o'clock. The extraordinary events that followed must be set down in Grimble's own words, as recounted in A *Pattern of Islands*:

Kuma was a big village in those days: its houses stretched for half a mile or more above the lagoon beach. The dreamer's hut lay somewhere near the centre of the line. The place was dead quiet that afternoon under its swooning palms. The children had been gathered in under the thatches. The women were absorbed in plaiting garlands and wreaths of flowers. The men were silently polishing their ceremonial ornaments of shell. Their friends from the west were being invited to a dance, and everything they did in the village that day was done to maintain the illusion.

Even the makings of a feast lay ready piled in baskets beside the houses. I could not bring myself to believe that the people expected nothing to come of all this careful business.

But the hot hours dragged by, and nothing happened. Four o'clock passed. My faith was beginning to sag under the strain when a strangled howl burst from the dreamer's hut. I jumped round to see his cumbrous body come hurtling head first through the torn screens. He sprawled on his face, struggled up, and staggered into the open, a slobber of saliva shining on his chin. He stood awhile clawing at the air and whining on a queer high note like a puppy's. Then words came gulping out of him: *"Teirake! Teirake!* (Arise! Arise!). . . . They come, they come! . . . Our friends from the west. . . . They come! Let us go down and greet them." He started at a lumbering gallop down the beach.

A roar went up from the village, "They come, they come!"

I found myself rushing helter-skelter with a thousand others into the shallows, bawling at the top of my voice that our friends from the west were coming. I ran behind the dreamer; the rest converged on him from north and south. We strung ourselves out, line abreast, as we stormed through the shallows. Everyone was wearing the garlands woven that afternoon. The farther out we got, the less the clamour grew. When we stopped, breast deep, fifty yards from the reef's edge, a deep silence was upon us; and so we waited.

I had just dipped my head to cool it when a man near me yelped and stood pointing; others took up his cry, but I could make out nothing for myself at first in the splintering glare of the sun on the water. When at last I did see them, everyone was screaming hard; they were pretty near by then, gambolling towards us at a fine clip. When they came to the edge of the blue water by the reef, they slackened speed, spread themselves out and started cruising back and forth in front of our line. Then, suddenly, there was no more of them.

In the strained silence that followed, I thought they were gone. The disappointment was so sharp, I did not stop to think then that, even so, I had seen a very strange thing. I was in the act of touching the dreamer's shoulder to take my leave when he turned his still face to me: "The king out of the west comes to meet me," he murmured, pointing downwards. My eyes followed his hand. There, not ten yards away, was the great shape of a porpoise poised like a glimmering shadow in the glass-green water. Behind it followed a whole dusky flotilla of them.

They were moving towards us in extended order with spaces of two or three yards between them, as far as my eye could reach. So slowly they came, they seemed to be hung in a trance. Their leader drifted in hard by the dreamer's legs. He turned without a word to walk beside it as it idled towards the shallows. I followed a foot or two behind its almost motionless

tail. I saw other groups to right and left of us turn shore-
wards one by one, arms lifted, faces bent upon the water.

A babble of quiet talk sprang up; I dropped behind to take
in the whole scene. The villagers were welcoming their guests
ashore with crooning words. Only men were walking beside
them; the women and children followed in their wake, clapping
their hands softly in the rhythm of a dance. As we approached
the emerald shallows, the keels of the creatures began to take
the sand; they flapped gently as if asking for help. The men
leaned down to throw their arms around the great barrels and
ease them over the ridges. They showed no least sign of alarm.
It was as if their single wish was to get to the beach.

When the water stood only thigh deep, the dreamer flung
his arms high and called. Men from either flank came crowding
in to surround the visitors, ten or more to each beast. Then,
"Lift!" shouted the dreamer, and the ponderous black shapes
were half-dragged, half-carried, unresisting, to the lip of the
tide. There they settled down, those beautiful, dignified shapes,
utterly at peace, while all hell broke loose around them. Men,
women and children, leaping and posturing with shrieks that
tore the sky, stripped off their garlands and flung them around
the still bodies, in a sudden dreadful fury of boastfulness and
derision. My mind still shrinks from that last scene—the
raving humans, the beasts so triumphantly at rest.

We left them garlanded where they lay and returned to our
houses. Later, when the falling tide had stranded them high
and dry, men went down with knives to cut them up. There
was feasting and dancing in Kuma that night.

Well, there it is. Useless to comment on this most extraordinary, and most tragic in its implications, of all dolphin
lore except to wonder whether there is not some connection
between the behavior of the Kuma dolphins and the earlier-
mentioned unexplained strandings of other cetaceans. Note

Grimble's statement, "It was as if their single wish was to get to the beach."

There was nothing strange in the fact that these dolphins displayed no fear when handled by the islanders. As early as 500 B.C. the Greeks were minting coins depicting boys riding on the backs of dolphins. And in the first century A.D. there is a description by Pliny the Younger of an incident that occurred at Hippo (now Bizerta) on the north coast of Africa, in which a dolphin joined some bathing boys and allowed one of them to ride on its back. For several days this dolphin, and on one occasion a companion, played with the boys. This incident, among others, was also referred to by the elder Pliny, who, having the curious mind of the true naturalist, paid for his curiosity when he approached Vesuvius too closely during the eruption of 79 A.D.

"Children's tales!" snorted the zoologists of the Victorian, Edwardian and Georgian eras. No one since the Romans had ever reported a dolphin playing with children or rescuing a drowning man. In any case it was inconceivable that a marine mammal could behave in such a way. They had heard, of course, of Pelorus Jack, but he (or she) associated only with ships, apparently attracted by the noise or vibrations of their engines, rubbing himself against a ship's plates and leaping and riding in its bow wave for twenty minutes at a time. And did not whales, porpoises and even sharks all commonly accompany ships?—though, unlike him, not regularly over a period of twenty-four years.

However, it is only fair to say that the true nature of the relationship of dolphins, and indeed of other cetaceans, with man is so incredible that no zoologist could be expected to believe it without the confirmation of contemporary evidence. And it is a relationship whose full potentialities are only now beginning to be realized. For almost two thousand years after the Romans, no scientific interest was taken in dolphins. Then, suddenly, Western man in general discovered that the sea was a good place to be in or near. And later, zoologists (or some of them) determined that the "lesser" mammals were not mere automatons responding mechanically to a given set of stimuli, but sentient beings.

The awakening began with a series of incidents during World War II, when an American airman reported that after he and five other members of his crew had bailed out into the Pacific, a dolphin had pushed their dinghy to the sandy beach of a small island.

In 1943, a woman bathing alone on a Florida beach panicked when caught in a strong undertow and was beginning to lose consciousness when "someone pushed me violently from behind and I landed on the beach with my nose in the sand, too exhausted to look round. When I was able to do so, there was no one near me, but in the water twenty feet from the shore, a dolphin was leaping and swimming in circles. A man came running over to me. He said that a dolphin had pushed me ashore."

Two years later another American, a thirteen-year-old girl swimmer, was being towed by a sailing boat when she was approached by a group of dolphins. After this initial encounter, she played with them every day, sometimes swimming with a dolphin on either side of her and a third in front. When she returned the following summer, she was again befriended by a group of six dolphins, one of which allowed her to hold on to its fin and be towed through the water.

No further incidents were reported during the next ten years, but early in 1955 a three-quarters-grown female bottle-nosed dolphin, possibly an orphaned yearling, began to follow small boats off Oponini, a beach and fishing village lying just within the harbor mouth of Hokianga on the west coast of New Zealand's North Island. "Opo," as she was called, was, like Pelorus Jack, was attracted by the sound or vibrations of boats' engines, especially those of outboard motors, and during the summer began to make distant acquaintance with human beings. Intimate contact was delayed until the following year, when a girl, again a gentle thirteen-year-old, not only played games with her but, like the boy in Pliny's "fable," regularly rode on her back. For two months Opo frolicked with the girl and other bathers, smacking her tail flat on the water in annoyance when the latter pestered her too much, before she was accidentally killed in March 1956.

Four years later fifty-one-year-old Yvonne Bliss fell overboard, unnoticed, one February night when her ship was in the Bahama Channel. After she had been in the water for a long time, a dolphin swam up behind her and, taking up position on her right side, prevented her from drifting with the current into deep and rough seas, while guiding her into shallow waters until her feet touched bottom.

The following year three men were reported to have been rescued by dolphins in Japanese waters after their motorboat had sunk; and in 1964 *Animals* magazine published the remarkable story of Nirumi Ikeda, a survivor from a Japanese fishing smack, the *South Sun*, which had gone down some way off the coast of the Awa-Kazusa peninsula the previous year. Since conditions prevented the launching of the smack's two lifeboats, six of the crew of ten were lost; and after six hours in the water the four survivors were near to drowning when, though no ship was in sight, they began to shout for help in desperation. Almost immediately two dolphins appeared, and Ikeda called out to another of the crew, Ogata, who was swimming a few yards behind him, "Those are dolphins. Aren't they the animals that rescue men?" Ikeda continues:

> Then I heard a gurgling sound. A dolphin was approaching me and puffing noisily. We were exhausted, and when the dolphin pushed us roughly aside and pressed us under water, Ogata cried: "He wants to kill us!"
> But then I clung on to the dolphin's back and dug my fingers into his flesh. This must have hurt the dolphin, but he let me continue doing it. He went on pressing the side of his body against mine, until I climbed on to his back as though I was mounting a horse. He started gurgling again. Then the dolphin swam with me on his back over to where Ogata was swimming, and shoved his side against Ogata's until he too climbed on to the dolphin's back. Minuro and Amatoka, the two other survivors, saw this, and the second dolphin seemed to be watching to see exactly what his bigger brother would do. Then the second dolphin performed the same manœuvre as his brother until eventually Minuro and Amatoka climbed on to his back. We hung, rather than sat, on the dolphins' backs, and they swam fast for 36 sea miles to the coast.

Ikeda concluded by describing how, when near the coast, both dolphins dumped their passengers into the sea with sharp jerks and then circled the men a few times while they swam the last few hundred yards to the shore, before leaping out to sea. Subsequently, these or other dolphins visited the Awa-Kazusa waters from time to time to play with the fishermen and be fed by them.

All the dolphins identified in these incidents have been

Tursiops, which, when full grown, is a large rotund dolphin, 10 or 11 feet in length, compared to the 8 feet of the slender *Delphinus* and the 12 or 13 feet of Risso's dolphin. Those commemorated by the Greeks and Romans seem to have been *Delphinus*, though it is predominantly an oceanic species in all warm and temperate seas, familiar to generations of sailors from its habit of playing around ships. In the tropics *Delphinus* schools may include a thousand or more individuals, who will race toward a ship in groups of ten or twenty and form up in all but solid layers in front of her bows and along her sides. It is natural that dolphins associating with human beings should be *Tursiops*, for it is mainly an inhabitant of coastal waters. But this species must include a number of geographical races, for its range includes not only the Pacific but the Atlantic coast of North America (where it is reported to be most numerous), the Mediterranean, the Bay of Biscay and the seas around the British Isles. Moreover, since the dolphins in the oceanariums of Florida and California prefer the temperature of their tanks to be between 80 and 85 degrees F, and do not thrive in water below 70 degrees F, they clearly cannot belong to the same race as those that visit the cool British seas. There, they occur most frequently in the southwestern approaches to the Channel. But if they enter the North Sea they do so by traveling up the west coast of England and around the north of Scotland.

In 1960 or 1961 a *Tursiops* adopted Elie, a fishing village on the Fifeshire coast of Scotland, as its home port. Charlie (who subsequently proved to be a female about 10 feet long) was to become well known to the fishermen of a number of villages on the Fife coast. She, like Opo, was attracted in the first place by boats, especially fast motorboats. And, as in other instances, it was a girl with whom she first made friends. But though the girl was allowed to pat Charlie on several occasions while the two were swimming around each other, she was never permitted to ride on her back.

In December 1964 Charlie disappeared from Fife waters. However, photographs showing her identification mark, a nick in the trailing edge of her dorsal fin, prove that she spent part of the summer of 1965 and most of 1966 off the Northumbrian fishing village of Seahouses, 70 miles to the south, and the following winter around the adjacent Farne Islands. In the meantime another dolphin had taken her place at Elie. Toward the end of April 1967, Charlie moved north again 30 miles, to Eyemouth, where she befriended and played with members of the local diving club (who were working on a wreck at a depth of about 40 feet) until early in December. She then disappeared and, since she suffered from a skin disease, may have died.

How are we to explain these superficially extraordinary approaches of wild dolphins to human beings disporting themselves or in difficulties in the seas of three different oceans? In the first place we must recognize that the relationship, from the dolphin's angle, has merely been one between two marine mammals and that to most *Tursiops* human mammals and their boats are familiar objects. Boat bottoms make excellent back-scratchers and also attract fish. Three aspects of dolphin mentality strike one immediately. They are highly intelligent, their herd ties are very strong, and they pass a great deal of their time in play, like most or all cetaceans, for even the great sperm whale will play with a floating plank. A motorboat scudding across the waves, children playing with a tire tube, or a girl splashing and diving with snorkel and fins, will arouse the curiosity of any playful dolphin. And Charlie's special delight was to roll alongside, and only a foot or two away from, an aquaplane being towed at a fair speed by a motorboat. There is no need to dwell at length upon the natural playfulness of dolphins, or upon the obvious enjoyment they display in their own games and in those devised by their keepers in oceanariums.

In those instances where it has been possible to determine their sex, dolphins playing with or rescuing human beings have been females, and it may be that maternalism influences their behavior. A dolphin's sex can be established only when it rolls over on its back and, if it is a female, reveals on either side of the vent the grooves that contain the teats. Because of this placing of the teats she is able, like a large whale, to suckle her single calf under water by squirting a large dose of extremely rich milk (containing six times the protein of human milk and considerably more fat) into its mouth on the instant that it touches a teat. That a female dolphin might find it quite natural to tow along a human mammal holding on to her fin is suggested by the fact that for several weeks after its birth the calf—which is suckled every half-hour night and day for the first two weeks—is almost as much a part of its mother as it was before it was born. It swims close beside her dorsal fin as if glued to it, with its outside eye closed, and as likely as not is protected on that side by one or more of the other females in the herd, who continue in close attendance for a couple of months or so. Should it be an individualist and repeatedly swim away from its mother, she may pin it to the bottom of the tank with her body for half a minute, or alternatively hold it above water for a full minute. In either case this treatment results in its subsequently swimming quietly by her side.

Another striking feature of dolphins' behavior is that they habitually help other members of the herd in difficulties.

Any dolphin, whether newborn calf or wounded adult, unable by its own efforts to rise to the surface for oxygen, is immediately raised and supported by its companions—another fact known to Aristotle. So compulsive is this urge to raise a helpless individual to the surface in order that it may breathe that on one occasion an exhausted porpoise, newly arrived at an oceanarium, was supported by a mixed group of *Tursiops* and Pacific striped dolphins. On another occasion a group of *Tursiops* was observed attempting with the greatest persistence to help a 5-foot leopard shark in this way, though since the latter is of course a fish this treatment was detrimental rather than helpful. Indeed, in a similar instance, a female *Tursiops* was actually responsible for the death of a leopard shark during the course of a day, by repeatedly forcing it above the surface with her snout. One would expect such an intelligent animal as a dolphin to be cognizant of the state of lifelessness. Yet, as in the case of

Bottle-nosed dolphins

one female who held her calf up to breathe for three days after its death, so for eight days, until the shark decomposed, this female continued to push its carcass to the surface, release it, and retrieve it again as soon as it sank, while permitting herself only the briefest off-periods in which to feed. In supporting a human mammal in difficulties, a dolphin would therefore be behaving in character, and its action is credible. Nor do only dolphins help each other in this way. An instance of sperm whales doing so has already been mentioned, and pilot whales, gray whales and humpbacks have all been observed supporting wounded companions.

That captive dolphins in an oceanarium should raise an unconscious newcomer which had struck its head on the side of the tank when being introduced to the surface, and then support it until it began breathing again, is in line with what we know of their natural behavior. But they are capable of more advanced therapeutic treatment than this. John C. Lilly gives a number of examples, including a remarkable case concerning a dolphin upon whom he had been conducting one of his experiments in the interests of scientific knowledge. In this particular experiment the dolphin was confined in a narrow tank of water at too low a temperature. The inactivity induced an S-shaped curve along its back. When it was returned to the main tank it was unable to flex its tail, and therefore unable to swim. As it began to sink it sounded its distress call—the customary crescendo-descrescendo of paired whistles. Immediately the two other dolphins in the tank swam to its aid and raised its head out of the water long enough for it to take in a gulp of air, but since it had still not recovered the use of its tail, it sank again. Lilly then heard over the hydrophone an exchange of whistles and twittering between the three of them. Then the two helpers adopted a different method of treatment, which continued for several hours. Instead of supporting the cripple's head, they now took turns in swimming at regular intervals beneath its ano-genital region and raked the sensitive external openings with their dorsal fins. This stimulated a downward reflex contraction of the powerful tail flukes and a consequent upward tilt of the head and blow-hole.

If the natural behavior of dolphins can be presumed to account for their playing with bathers and assisting swimmers in difficulties, it cannot fully explain those incidents in which a dolphin pushed a dinghy with six American airmen to land and when two dolphins carried four Japanese fishermen on their backs for 36 sea miles. Assuming that these incidents have been more or less correctly reported, they are barely explicable by any level of intelligence. For put yourself in the place of these dolphins. How would you deduce that a boatload of men, or swimmers in the sea, required assistance and that they wished to be taken to land? Or are these incidents to be regarded merely as fortuitous extensions of a dolphin's perpetual pursuit of fun and games, whether these be expressed in carrying children on one's back or teaming up with one's fellows to push a waterlogged mattress to shore?

A deeper understanding of the relationship between dolphins and man is provided by the behavior of tame and captive dolphins. All mammals have retentive memories; but it is perhaps worth recording that when Robert Stenuit returned to the Marineland of Miami after an absence of eighteen months, a male *Tursiops*, approaching maturity, stared at him for a long time with head held high out of the water and mouth half open, while treading water with paddling tail. Then, ignoring the other spectators, he swam away to fetch the same rubber ring with which he and Stenuit had previously played, looped it over his beak, swam back to Stenuit, and threw it into his hands. Dolphins learn very much more quickly than monkeys, and possibly as quickly as human beings. And the games played by immature dolphins in oceanariums demonstrate that, in Anthony Alpers' words, they have the intellectual capacity of a man to premeditate an action, develop an idea, and maintain sustained interest in an activity. It is significant that if the games devised for them by their keepers are not sufficiently complex, and are not changed from time to time, they lose interest in them. And the very fact that they become bored must contribute toward their excellence as performers of a wide variety of tricks and games.

Numerous examples of dolphins' ability to work out a solution to a problem have been observed among those in captivity. Consider in particular the activities of two male *Tursiops* in a California oceanarium. These were attempting to pull a moray eel out of its crevice between two rocks on the bottom of the pool by stationing themselves at either end of the crevice and working the eel back and forth. However, since this technique proved unsuccessful, one of the dolphins eventually swam away and killed a newly introduced scorpion fish with a blow from its beak into the latter's belly, which is the only unprotected part of this 12-inch fish armed with sharp, poisonous dorsal spines. Then, returning to the crevice, it poked at the eel with the fish, apparently prodding it with the spines and causing it to shoot out of the crevice into open water, where it was caught. But instead of killing the eel, the dolphin released it in the middle of the pool. Since dolphins are not known to eat moray eels, it is a reasonable assumption that this particular one had been selected as a plaything. But since it is also extremely unlikely that they eat the poisonous scorpion fish, was the dolphin aware of the probable effect of its spines on the eel?

Dolphins in captivity never sleep, but rest for a few minutes at a time (totaling two hours out of the twenty-four) while hanging near the surface with flukes depressed, rising slowly to breathe, then sinking again. With so many idle hours to occupy in every twenty-four, since they do not have to hunt for food, it is possible that *Tursiops* in captivity release some of their frustration in sexuality, for the males are not only in almost perpetual pursuit of the females, who come into heat a few times a year, but attempt to mate with virtually any animate object, whether this be skate, bat ray, leopard shark, green turtle, moray eel or human diver—to the embarrassment of all and sundry.

There is another aspect of the relationship between dolphins and man. It has not escaped notice that a full understanding of a dolphin's marvelous sonic apparatus would be of vital military value, and the United States' annual budget for dolphin research by naval technicians amounts to the incredible figure of almost $1,000,000. The research is concentrated primarily on *Tursiops*, whose sonic abilities and intelligence have attracted so much attention in oceanariums and laboratories, and who apparently enjoys some aspects of life in captivity—that is, if this sensitive animal survives the extreme shock of capture and the initial days of starvation while it is being "tamed." If I read between the lines of various oceanarium reports correctly, there appears to be a considerable mortality among dolphins during and after capture. Indeed, the representatives from ten different countries attending the First International Symposium on Cetacean Research in 1963 were extremely frank on this point. The current worldwide craze of urban authorities for pepping up their home towns with dolphinaria—substituting performing dolphins for circus lions and tigers—must therefore be viewed with some concern.

The oceanic common and striped dolphins naturally take less kindly to small enclosures and are also less flexible in their movements and less curious about man's activities. Some common dolphins, after several days of solitary confinement, may either drown themselves or ram their heads repeatedly against the wall of their pool—again, this awkward implication of cetacean suicide. And who can be surprised at this behavior after reading Cousteau's account of the joyous corporate activities of a great herd of common dolphins?

> Some miles ahead, there was a barrier of foam across the horizon. . . . Half a mile from it we saw that the splashing breakers were composed of leaping dolphins, the most formidable host that . . . I had seen in a quarter of a century at sea. . . . The dolphin army wheeled and charged toward us in a storm comber that erupted twisting black bodies in the air . . . shooting vertically out of the water, bending and contorting in the leap. . . .
>
> For the rest of the day *Calypso* was steered by dolphins, obeying the whims of the flying phalanx spreading before us to either rim of the ocean. . . . The tails were clearing the water by twelve to fifteen feet. As they fell, they twisted into awkward postures. . . . At a given minute, there were about a thousand out of the water in jumps that averaged three seconds. For one in the air, there must have been nineteen in the water. Perhaps twenty thousand dolphins formed the living reef.

From the underwater chamber the sight was apocalyptic. The radius of transparency was about a hundred feet, a sphere packed with streaming bodies effortlessly maintaining the pace of *Calypso*. Some dolphins hung close to the windows of the observatory, intimately eyeing the men inside. The escort was criss-crossed by dolphins charging across the bow with flickering speed. Through this fleeting, cross-hatching pack there was also an astounding vertical movement. Dolphins sped straight up from the deep, threw themselves into a sort of rocket-booster stage in front of the windows, and shot through the glittering ceiling. They belly-flopped back into the water, collected themselves and sounded, printing a white trail of exhalations in the blue.*

In the experiments conducted in 1965 by naval technicians at the United States research station Sealab 2, 200 feet under the sea off La Jolla, California, the research team was working in exceptionally murky waters. Visibility was rarely more than 10 feet and at times no more than arm's length, and there was a considerable danger of a diver being lost when working at any distance from the station. Therefore the help of an immature *Tursiops*, 6½ feet long and 300 pounds in weight, was enlisted. "Tuffy" had been previously trained to respond to the signal of an electric buzzer strapped to a diver's forearm, and it was his duty to dive down to the station from his holding-pen beside a boat on the surface, pick up the end of a line from a spool and swim with it to a "lost" diver, delivering it into his hand. Released in the open sea, Tuffy was free to swim away and resume a natural exist-

* Abridged and adapted from p. 123 of *The Living Sea* by Jacques-Yves Cousteau, with James Dugan. Copyright © 1963 by Harper & Row, Publishers, Incorporated. Reprinted by permission of Harper & Row, Publishers, Inc.

ence with other dolphins, but, as Michael Greenwood has described in *Animals* magazine, he never made any attempt to do so. He remained on call and dove willingly to the station when required, ignoring the dense shoals of fish attracted by the latter's floodlights. Nor did he ever display any hesitation about returning to the boat when his trainer buzzed for him. He was, however, so disturbed and repelled by the sounds emanating from the station that he would not go close to it. This difficulty was surmounted by placing a diver with the spool at some distance from the station. When the "lost" diver sounded his buzzer, Tuffy would dive down to the bottom immediately, pick up the line from one diver and rush it across to the other, who would feed him the cut of frozen fish he had been accustomed to receive during training. Greenwood wrote: "Tuffy would wait patiently for you to take the line from him, in fact he would positively put it into your hand and continue to nudge you until you grasped it firmly. When he was assured that you had the line he expected his just reward. If it was not immediately forthcoming he would utter a high scream of indignation, and even remind you of your obligation by spanking you with his tail."

Tuffy not only displayed remarkable ability in finding a lost diver, but demonstrated that he could also deliver tools and act as a general messenger between the surface personnel and the station's divers. A postscript to the experiments with Tuffy was provided by a wild sea lion that also learned voluntarily to respond to the divers' calls, leaving his herd and homing on the buzzer from distances of 600 yards or more, to be rewarded by a meal of frozen fish.

And a false killer whale (a dolphin) at the Hawaiian Oceanic Foundation has been trained to do a "Tuffy," carrying compressed-air drills and heavy sledgehammers in a nylon sling held in her mouth to divers working 20 feet down on the bottom of the tank.

The brain of a *Tursiops* is of the same order of complexity and almost as large as a man's, taking into account their relative body-lengths, and more than twice as large as a gorilla's. Whether extensive development of the cerebrum and cerebellum indicates exceptional intellectual ability, or alternatively a strongly centralized nervous system controlling the senses, has not been established. But there cannot be any doubt about the advanced intelligence of an animal who can be instructed by another dolphin (hidden from it, but within hearing) to push one correct lever out of several in order to receive a fish. And this when the instructor dolphin itself is directed by light signals to the correct lever that will activate similar signals in the other dolphin's compartment.

At the present time it seems that the dolphins are the most exciting inhabitants of the ocean because of their intellectual potentialities, while their relatives the great whales are the most awe-inspiring. But perhaps this will remain true only until we learn more about the capabilities of porpoises and whales, should this ever prove feasible in the case of the larger whales.

Cousteau was somewhat dismayed to discover that not only did a porpoise's lungs resemble his own, but that its brain was as large as his, and that it was deeply corrugated in the manner that was supposed to indicate human genius. In fact the brains of porpoises, white whales and narwhals are actually more highly developed than those of dolphins. In captivity, pilot whales become friendly with man in a shorter time than dolphins and have been considered as promising subjects for naval training.

The brain of a true killer whale is seven times heavier than that of an elephant, and there can be little doubt that it is highly intelligent. Though generally presented as the frenetic scourge of the ocean, killers in captivity are extraordinarily gentle, not only taking fish from the hand and allowing their keepers to ride on their backs, but actually performing with dolphins, their natural prey, in the same tank. It is perhaps significant that the nineteenth-century whalers of New South Wales were as emphatic that killers helped them to capture humpbacked whales as the fishermen of the Mediterranean, Florida and California still are that dolphins assist them by herding shoals of fish toward their boats. According to Anthony Alpers, when a humpback had been harpooned, some members of the attendant pack of killers would perform a concerted and peculiar action :

> Four of the killers separate from the rest, and whilst two of them station themselves beneath the head of the whale, so preventing her from sounding, the others swim side by side, from time to time throwing themselves out of the water on top of her and right across her blow-hole. They are speedily thrown off again, but the action is continued, as if the killers were well aware that by so doing they hindered the breathing of the whale.

Possibly they are able to kill only harpooned whales, and their ability to kill such large animals as blue whales may have been exaggerated, for observers in the spotter aircraft employed by whaling companies state that bull blue whales have no difficulty in driving off packs of killers attacking the cows and calves in a herd, and there have also been reports of humpback bulls driving away killers with blows of their tail flukes in similar circumstances. But killers certainly cooperate when hunting in couples or in packs of up to forty. Off Baja California a pack of fifteen to twenty killers has been observed circling a herd of a hundred dolphins, gradually hemming them in more and more closely, until finally one killer cleaves in and kills a dolphin, while the rest of the pack continues circling. Then one killer after another breaks formation, kills a dolphin, and returns to its place.

According to Eskimos a pair of killers will press against either side of a narwhal until its ribs cave in, and Prince Albert of Monaco has described how, when he was harpooning one of a pack of four killers, the harpoon passed right through it and wounded another, whereupon the other two came alongside his boat and repeatedly attempted to squeeze it between them. In this they were thwarted by the carcass of their harpooned companion, which had been hauled up and served as a fender on one side of the boat, and also by the rounded lines of the hull and of the killers themselves, which resulted in the boat's being "squeezed" out of the water instead of compressed.

One cannot conclude this account of killer whales without asking what unknown factor controls their numbers and prevents them from increasing excessively. It can hardly be argued in their case that carnivores can never become more numerous than the available prey, because their prey includes any large-enough fish or mammal, though particularly squids perhaps, in all the world's oceans, providing that it is in active motion; sea otters are reported to freeze in order to escape detection.

Killer whales may be dolphins' only significant predators. Though sharks certainly kill some, it was Captain Young's experience in seas around the globe that only the large Australian tiger sharks preyed regularly on dolphins. However, in the Marineland of Miami, Florida, *Tursiops* has been on exhibition since 1938, with the exception of a four-year hiatus during World War II, the herd swims in a tight defensive formation, with the cows and calves in its middle. And at the birth of a calf the mother is surrounded by other females, who ward off not only too inquisitive males, but also any sharks that may be attracted by the slight mist of blood when the umbilical cord is broken. The to-all-appearances unarmed dolphins are by no means defenseless. In the Gulf of Mexico they are reported to chase sharks out of their fishing waters, and there have been a number of instances, both in captivity and in their natural element, of groups of dolphins killing such formidable predators as tiger sharks and hammerheads by charging them at high speed and punching them in the most sensitive parts of the belly or in the region of the gills with a series of rapid, jolting blows from their hard, bony beaks. Several members of a herd may maneuver a shark into the right position for it to be struck in a critical place by another dolphin. In one oceanarium a male *Tursiops* was seen to swim up at considerable speed and strike a 5-foot leopard-shark in the mid-body with its beak. Although the shark almost doubled up with the force of the impact, it was apparently unharmed. When ramming a shark, the dolphin's lower jaw is locked to the upper, and the shock is transmitted to the very thick forehead and absorbed by the powerful neck muscles. Since a shark's skeleton is composed of cartilage or gristle, it lacks the protection of a rib cage, and such vital organs as the liver are easily crushed by an external blow.

We have already noted the extraordinary gentleness of killer whales, both true and false. And one of the most remarkable aspects of the numerous associations of dolphins with human beings, whether in captivity or in the sea, is that never under any provocation has one retaliated roughly enough to inflict any injury. As far as I am aware, the only recorded instance of aggression occurred when a herd of ten attacked some Porto Garibaldi fishermen who had caught one of their number in their nets.

15: Migration Problems

On one occasion, when Cousteau was 40 miles out in the Atlantic, with the coast of North Africa far out of sight, and his boat traveling at 12 knots, a school of porpoises came up from astern and overtook the *Elie Monnier*. After running with them for a while, on a direct bearing for the Strait of Gibraltar, Cousteau altered course five or six degrees in an attempt to deflect them. For a few minutes they accepted this alteration, but then swung away from the bows of the boat, and when Cousteau followed them he found that they were again headed on a direct bearing for the Strait. He wrote, "Wherever they came from, the porpoises had secure knowledge of where the ten-mile gate lay in the immense sea."

Thousands of whales, dolphins and porpoises migrate seasonally through the Strait of Gibraltar. An inherited knowledge of the route to be taken, currents and temperature gradients, the "taste" of different waters, the position of the sun and the stars—the significance of some or perhaps all of these navigational aids may be registered by their huge brains simultaneously and instantaneously. But sonar must surely play a vital part, informing them by its echoes of the nature, and the distance from them, of the rugged sea bottom, particularly in deep or murky waters where any navigational aid the sun might give would be lost. Swimming at 5,000 feet above the bottom, they would receive the bounce-back echo 2 seconds after signaling.

Fish also undertake migrations involving voyages of hundreds or thousands of miles. Schools of cod regularly migrate 700 miles from their feeding grounds in the Arctic to their spawning grounds off the Lofoten Islands, while, as examples of long-distance individual migrations, two blue-fin tunnies tagged off the coast of Florida were caught off Bergen (4,500 miles distant by the most direct route) four months later. Subsequently, ten more from Florida waters were recovered in the Bay of Biscay, while a further five, and also an albacore, migrated more than 5,000 miles from Californian waters to the sea of Japan. But neither fish nor eels nor turtles have sonic equipment, though fish with lateral-line senses must be held to have limited echo-ranging powers, because the energy waves set in motion by a swimming fish flow outward in all directions and are reflected back by any object they encounter. How, then, do fish, eels and turtles orientate across the Atlantic and the Pacific?

At some time in the distant past some green turtles made use of the beaches of Ascension Island as suitable repositories for their eggs, despite the fact that the nearest beds of turtle grass (Thalassia), their staple food, lay 1,000 miles to the north off the Guinea coast of Africa or 1,300 miles to the west off South America, as the gull flies. Although green turtles are not exclusively vegetarian and will feed voraciously on shell-less flying snails and small lobsters, one must presume that they could not survive for any length of time without turtle grass, and that the founders of the Ascension colony reached the island accidentally—perhaps with the south equatorial current which flows from east to west in this latitude. However, having laid their eggs but found no *Thalassia* beds, they were obliged to move on. Whether these adult turtles returned to Africa against the equatorial current, or swam on with it to South America, does not concern us. What does concern us is that when the young turtles hatched they had no option but to be carried with the current eventually to the vast fields of turtle-grass off Brazil. Yet, although the coasts of South and Central America, and of the Caribbean Islands, are amply supplied with suitable laying beaches for turtles, we are not in the least surprised to find that when these young African turtles reached sexual maturity, they ignored these and set forth against the currents on the 1,300-mile return migration to their birthplace on Ascension. The impelling urge to return to the birth or home territory is the basis of the phenomenon of migration, whether it be that of mammal, bird, fish or reptile.

Whether or not this is a correct hypothesis is, again, unimportant. What is important is that numbers of green turtles, tagged while laying their eggs on Ascension, have frequently been recovered in the *Thalassia* fields off Brazil; and that their tags indicate that they undertake this egg-laying migration every two or three years, or at longer intervals. But how did the original young African turtles find their way back from South America to Ascension? Even if they retained a memory of the westward route during the years that they were maturing in Brazilian waters, they would have had to reconstruct it in reverse. One is forced to fall back upon the

Female green sea turtle

existence of some form of hereditary memory—a term as imprecise and uninformative as the term "instinct," though undoubtedly a stock possession of a wide variety of animals.

However, turtles, like other animals, are able to "home" under conditions in which hereditary memory can play no part. Consider the feat of one particular green turtle. Caught on the Mosquito Bank off Nicaragua, and branded with the skipper's private mark, it was dispatched by schooner to the market at Key West off the southern horn of Florida, a distance of more than a thousand miles by the shortest sea passage. But before it could be sold, a hurricane washed it out of the Key West holding-pens. Eight months later this branded turtle, additionally distinguished by certain physical peculiarities, was again caught on the Mosquito Bank by the same skipper. In coastal waters a turtle or a fish can no doubt find its way around by such aids as the "taste" of different waters and currents, or by familiar submarine sea marks. But this turtle, whose movements had previously been restricted to a daily 4- or 5-mile swim between the coral head or rock on or under which it rested at night, and the shallow waters of its particular field of narrow-leaved turtle grass, had been able to navigate many hundreds of miles across strong currents and through presumably unknown channels between the Caribbean islands.

Even assuming the possession of a hereditary memory, how does a turtle, or a sea bird for that matter, orientate physically to a small oceanic island, a mere speck hundreds or perhaps thousands of miles from the nearest land? Such an island, surrounded by water thousands of feet deep, cannot be located by its odor as a river might be, nor by compass sense alone. It is reasonably certain that a migrant bird, equipped with a light-compass and an internal clock, is able to determine its course, and to correct its heading when forced off course, by celestial navigation from the sun and the stars, and possibly the moon; though one must add that its ability to navigate is not necessarily dependent on any of these aids. But neither turtle nor fish could locate an island by this means because,

Consider also the precision clocks with which such lowly inhabitants of shallow continental waters as palolo worms and grunions are equipped. The former, which are relatives of the fireworms, are several inches long, the males colored light brown and ocher, the females grayish-indigo and green. They inhabit burrows in dead coral and during immaturity are repelled by light, whether sunlight or pale moonlight, venturing out of their burrows only in the darkest hours to feed on algae. But as the season of spawning approaches and the posterior third of their bodies becomes distended with eggs or sperm, light becomes a stimulus instead of a repellent. At high water of the lowest tides, on the night before (or within three nights before) the moon reaches its last quarter in June and July in the West Indies and off the Gilbert Islands in the Pacific, in October and November off Samoa and Fiji, and on the second and third nights after the full moon in March and April in the Malay Archipelago, the palolos back out of their burrows two hours or more before sunrise, twisting and writhing with spiraling antics until the distended tail portions break off and wriggle up to the surface. In the palolos of Japanese waters it is the forepart that breaks away on the nights immediately following new and full moons in October and November. Then, when the first rays of the sun strike the sea at dawn, the "tails" again begin to twist and contract with violent spasms, and finally burst, discoloring the sea with vast quantities of eggs and sperm. (But do clouds never obscure the sun at this critical juncture?) For a short while after spawning, the deflated tail-bags continue to wriggle weakly, until those not gobbled up by the shoals of fish attracted by this feast die and sink. Within three hours after sunrise, all have disappeared. But by the evening of this same day minute, spirally swimming larvae have hatched from the eggs, and after about three days in surface waters these wriggle down to take possession of burrows in the reefs, where the foreparts of their parents are in the process of regenerating new tails, which will become reproductively ripe the next year—as will the larvae.

It could be argued that in order to conform to this annual mating calendar the palolos must possess a timing mechanism that will take account not only of the 24.8-hour lunar day (measured from moonrise to moonrise), but also of the 29.5-day synodical month (from full moon to full moon). Laboratory experiments indeed indicate that it is not the state of the tides that activates the palolos, and one must presume that they respond to those obscure lunar rhythms which appear to influence so many of the ocean's inhabitants—and not only those of the ocean, for what impells the armies of land crabs to migrate annually from the mountains of Savaii, Samoa's largest island, to the seashore three days before the swarming of the palolos upon which they feed?

Grunions are small fish from 5 to 9 inches long, whose breeding season extends from late February to early September; but their actual spawning runs, as observed on the beaches of California south of Monterey, are restricted to the first, second, third or fourth nights after the highest spring tide of the series at the new or full moon. No two observers give identical accounts of the spawning procedure; but about a quarter of an hour after the crest of the tide, shortly before it begins to recede, and when the moon is well above the horizon, the first shoals of grunions ride ashore in their thousands on each breaking wave, and swim up the gently sloping beach almost as far as the wash reached, until their backs are actually out of the water. For an hour or more their multitudes arrive and depart; while in the 20 or 30 seconds between the receding of their transporting wave and the onrush of the next, or even between the arrival and ebbing of one wave, the females squirm and wriggle, tail-first, a couple of inches down into the sand about 12 inches below the highest point reached by any wave. Then, when in an almost vertical position, they stir the sand with tails and fins, rendering it soft and fluid, and shed their two thousand eggs. When they are buried up to their pectorals, the one or more males, which have been lying quietly beside each female, loop themselves around her and fertilize the eggs. During the next few days successively lower tides pile up the sand over the grunions' burrows to a depth of from 3 to 12 inches, and after ten days or so the surface of the sand has dried out. This may perhaps serve as a protective measure, though a proportion of the eggs are discovered by such wading birds as sanderlings. The embryos in the eggs are normally fully developed within seven days, so that when the next spring tide cuts down the beach a couple of weeks after the spawning and the eggs are ruptured by the vibration of the surf, the grunion fry are prepared within three minutes for life in the ocean. Laboratory experiments have confirmed the fact that the fully developed embryos will hatch only when the eggs are shaken, as they are in the natural state by the rolling surf.

We can now appreciate that if the grunions spawned just before the highest springs the chances are that the beach might be further eroded and the eggs washed out before they had developed. If they spawned with the highest tide at the new moon, the eggs might not be exposed by equally high tides for one, or possibly two, months; but by spawning on the ebbing tides following the highest, they ensure—barring unpredictable storm tides—that the next spring tides will reach the interim period varies from one to as long as seven years, there is some circumstantial evidence that such a memory may be possible. Computerized data indicates, for example, that 37 per cent of a sample of American salmon, homing at random without any special navigational aids, would make a landfall within a 40-mile radius of their hereditary spawning rivers; the deduction being again that thereafter they would be able to home on the odor of their particular river from that distance. But that such odors could be disseminated by currents for distances of up to 2,500 miles between the salmon at sea and their spawning rivers is not credible; and we do not know by what means the adults orientate to these, or how the smolts locate the hereditary feeding waters of their kind.

However, there is one hard fact about fish migration that is indisputable—namely, that it is standard procedure for the adults to travel and orientate against the prevailing currents to their spawning grounds. Cod and herrings in the eastern North Atlantic swim against the currents to their spawning grounds, and so do the dog salmon (a Pacific salmon) when entering the Sea of Okhotsk to spawn in the Amur. This procedure ensures that their fry will have the option of traveling fortuitously downcurrent to the traditional feeding grounds of their kind. Both smolts and young sea trout are known to swim for weeks with the currents, and this practice would appear to offer the only logical explanation of a fish's ability to orientate across the featureless ocean, though it must be admitted that smolts migrating from British rivers to the recently discovered feeding grounds of salmon in Greenland waters would first have to extricate themselves from the north-flowing Arctic extension of the Gulf Stream in order to enter the westerly drift to the south of Iceland—unless, of course, they make use of favorable submarine currents flowing at various levels and at present uncharted.

The other classic transoceanic migrant is the common freshwater eel, whose only known spawning grounds, whether its nationality be North American, European or North African, are in the deeps of the Sargasso Sea between 55° and 68° West and some hundreds of miles to the south of Bermuda. Their precise location is not known, for spawn has never been found, either floating or attached to sargassum weed, and this is also true of those freshwater eels which go out to spawn in west Pacific and Indo-Pacific deeps. But since the smallest larvae of the Atlantic eels have been netted at a depth of 1,000 feet, the eggs no doubt rise, like those of so many fish, from greater depths. However that may be, Johannes Schmidt's hypothesis of the eel larvae's life history has been almost universally accepted. This indicated that the young eels begin to deploy from the Sargasso spawning-deep when still transparent larvae 2/5th inch long. Having risen to a depth of around 600 feet, where the sun's influence is felt, they are carried by the Gulf Stream and other North Atlantic currents to widely separated destinations. Some reach the rivers of eastern North America, as far north as Labrador, after a voyage of more than 1,000 miles and of one year's duration. Others travel to the rivers of western Europe, from Iceland and arctic Norway in the north to the Mediterranean and northwest Africa in the south, after voyages of from 2,000 to 3,000 miles, lasting three years. Schmidt's series of netting stations across the Atlantic indicated that by the end of their first summer the larvae have traveled 400 miles and have grown to a length of 1 inch. By the end of the second year, when they have grown another inch, they have risen to within 80 or 160 feet of the surface of the mid-

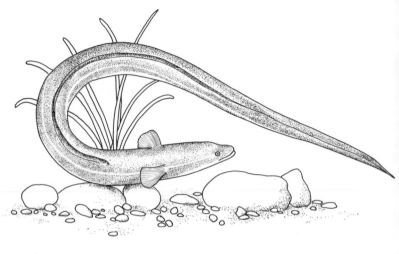

Common eel

Atlantic. At the end of the third year, when between 2½ and 3 inches long, they reach European coasts and change from transparent larvae into elvers recognizable as young eels. The rivers will be their home for periods varying from five to eight and a half years while, feeding voraciously, they grow to maturity. Exceptional individuals remain in the rivers until they are twenty or thirty years old.

The age of an eel can be estimated by growth rings on the scales that begin to form when the elvers enter the rivers. Fish's powers of regeneration are so much greater than those of mammals that they might be described theoretically as immortal. Cod are known to survive for more than twenty years and plaice for the quite unbelievable time of sixty years, while a sturgeon may still be growing after seventy years. One 14-foot Russian beluga sturgeon weighing 1 ton was estimated to be seventy-five years old, and a rather smaller American sturgeon eighty-two years old. What age are sturgeons weighing more than a ton and half? Are they fish of fantastic longevity, or have they grown to this colossal size as a result of exceptionally favorable food and habitat?

Schmidt built up his odyssey of the eels' migrations by netting ever-increasing sizes of larvae at various stations eastward across the Atlantic, and there would seem to be no doubt that eels in the rivers on both sides of the Atlantic all originate in the Sargasso spawning-deeps. Nevertheless, very awkward questions have not been answered. As knowledgeable a marine biologist as Sir Alister Hardy has pointed out that we do not even know if the eggs of eels from, say, Scottish rivers are fertilized by Scottish male eels. However, assuming that this is the case, what possible selective ocean drifting from the Sargasso can carry larvae of Scottish stock 2,000 miles across the Atlantic to Scotland, while at the same time carrying the larvae of Spanish stock to Spain? The only solution to this problem would seem to be that there are in fact no separate geographical stocks of eels, but that the billions of larvae rising out of the considerable spawning area in the Sargasso deploy at random into various currents that eventually deposit them at random points up and down the coasts on either side of the Atlantic. But if there are no geographical races, then why are all American eels physically distinct from those in Europe and North Africa in possessing from 104 to 110 vertebrae, whereas the latter possess from 111 to 119? This distinction need not, however, necessarily be a racial one, for there is experimental evidence that the number of vertebrae in such fish as sea trout and herrings can be influenced by a sudden change in the temperature of the water into which they rise shortly after hatching. Denys

W. Tucker has suggested that eels are also affected in this way, those hatching in one area of the Sargasso rising into waters of a different temperature from that of another area. At the same time those in the first area rise into a current system that will carry them up the Eastern Seaboard of North America, while those in the second area rise into currents that will drift them across the Atlantic.

Tucker takes this argument a revolutionary step further, asserting that there are no geographical races of eels because all are in fact the produce of a single stock of American eels spawning in different areas of the Sargasso and rising into different current systems. This is an attractive hypothesis, because the most puzzling of all the enigmas in the eels' life history is the fact that no adults have ever been captured anywhere near the Sargasso Sea. Indeed, none have ever been captured beyond the limits of the continental shelf a few score miles off the coasts of Europe and North Africa. On one hand, therefore, it seems indisputable that the eels' only spawning area is the Sargasso. On the other hand, there is the inexplicable fact that after years of concentrated search for an adult eel traveling westward across the Atlantic to spawn, the only possible such record is the recent discovery of two small females (less than 18 inches long) in migratory condition in the stomachs of two fish, trawled at a depth of around 700 feet some 150 miles northwest of St. Kilda. Yet it is also indisputable that when eels mature they go down the rivers to the sea. During the later summer or in the autumn they stop feeding, a fundamental change associated with the shrinking and degeneration of their digestive organs and the complementary development of their internal sex organs. At the same time their thyroid and pituitary glands increase in activity, their skins thicken and change color from yellow to silver with the acquisition of guanine pigments, their swim-bladders decrease in size, and their eyes become four times as large and acquire those golden pigments in the retina which we have seen to be characteristic of midwater fish. In short, in preparation for what one would presume to be their transoceanic voyage to the Sargasso spawning-deep, they are patently undergoing the necessary metamorphosis from a freshwater fish into a deep-water marine one. Though by what means they could orientate 2,000 or 3,000 miles to one particular ocean deep they left as barely sensate larvae at least eight years earlier, one cannot begin to understand. Quite so, says Tucker; but though your European eels certainly leave their rivers and enter the sea, they die shortly after doing so and will never spawn in the Sargasso or anywhere else. Their stock will be replenished by a new generation of elvers spawned by American eels. This is an ingenious argument, which cannot be refuted until a marked adult is captured within a reasonable range of the Sargasso spawning area. One must, however, ask why European eels should prepare themselves for a marine existence if they are to die within a few days or weeks of entering the sea, and why the females' ovaries should be developing when they leave the rivers.

The problems presented by the migratory voyages of eels and turtles, fish and whales will never be solved, as Robert Ardrey says, until science accomplishes some major penetration into areas of perception at present unknown. For the present we can only continue to grope through our own muddy waters.

16: Harvest from the Seas

It has been widely and authoritatively stated that when the harvest from the earth's farms and fields is no longer adequate to feed mankind's proliferating millions they will not starve, because there are greater potential supplies of food in the oceans than any foreseeable human population could make use of. This optimistic forecast assumes, first, that we can assess the probable numbers of human beings at any given time in the future, which we cannot do; second, that we are technically able to harvest this potential supply of sea-food, which at present we are unable to do; third, that we do not put this potential harvest in jeopardy by overfishing, over-killing and polluting marine life. Overfishing and overkilling we have in fact been doing at an ever-increasing rate for three hundred years, slaughtering whales and seals to the verge of extinction and exploiting traditional fishing grounds to the extent that during the past decade the total catch of the world's fishing fleets has actually declined, despite enormous landings by the new fleets of such nations as Peru and the USSR.

But a much graver threat to the oceans' existing stocks of fish and other marine life than that of overfishing is the relatively recent phenomenon of pollution—pollution by tanker oil, by industrial and urban effluents, by agricultural fertilizers, weed-killers and pesticides, by seepage from dumpings of war chemicals and no doubt, in due course, of nuclear waste. Even marine biologists were probably not fully aware of how widely the sea was polluted until 1970, when Thor Heyerdahl crossed the Atlantic from northwest Africa to Barbados in his papyrus-reed boat *Ra II*, and Cousteau subsequently completed a three-and-a-half-year research voyage of 155,000 miles through the world's oceans. On reaching Barbados, Heyerdahl reported that *Ra II* had passed through clumps of oil on almost every one of the fifty-seven days of the 3,000-mile crossing, and that in some places the sea was so unbelievably fouled with oil that the crew had found it impossible to bathe. Cousteau confirmed this ocean-wide pollution. Since both explorers were voyaging far from the main shipping routes, it is evident that the currents are disseminating oil and other pollutants over vast areas of ocean. We also know that persistent poisonous chemicals are being transferred along the food chain of prey and predators to the farthest bounds of ocean, for residues of DDT have been found in the organs of Antarctic penguins.

At the conclusion of his voyage Cousteau is reported as stating that during the past twenty years marine life has diminished by 40 per cent and that the oceans are dying. Though these are presumably in the nature of informed guesses on his part, they certainly do not overstress the menace of pollution. Yet there are still irresponsible scientist who can talk glibly of employing nuclear power to remove undersea obstructions in order to create harbors or to heat polar waters in order to improve the climate in parts of the Northern Hemisphere. I think we have learned enough in the preceding chapters of the delicate ecological inter-relationships in the sea, particularly those of plankton, to conceive of the consequences should nuclear power be used in this way.

It is against this background of persistent overfishing, and especially of pollution, that we have to consider whether in fact the oceans can supply the colossal quantities of food required to support indefinitely millions or tens of millions of human beings. We must assume, in the first place, that even if fully adequate conservation measures are introduced in the immediate future, pollution will continue to increase substantially for some years to come. It is optimistic in the extreme to suppose that mankind could suddenly stop pollution. However, we will be optimistic and put our faith in nature's proven ability to recover from near catastrophes. Some species of whales and seals, for example, have appeared to be in imminent danger of extermination, and yet after a few years' protection have increased in numbers dramatically.

Most advocates of the theory that mankind's hungry millions can be fed by the sea have been attracted by the potentialities of plankton. These, as we have seen, occur in inconceivable numbers, though not, it must be stressed, uniformly throughout the oceans. Estimates of the world's stock of plankton can be disregarded as little more than guesses, but their total mass must amount to billions of tons. Well and good, but how do you harvest substantial quantities of organisms so minute that the fine-mesh nets used by marine biologists retain only about a quarter of the potential catch? Moreover, in order to obtain 1 pound dry weight of plankton it would be necessary to filter about a million gallons of water. Clearly, extraordinary technical problems would have to be surmounted before plankton could be harvested in realistic quantities.

That being the case, would it be possible to harvest the comparatively large krill? They constitute about half the total mass of plankton in the Antarctic, and perhaps 50 million tons—approximately the annual weight of fish landed by the world's fishing fleets—or perhaps considerably more could be fished. Sir Alister Hardy was at one time enthusiastic about the possibilities of harvesting krill with machines simulating whales cruising open-mouthed through the masses, but that was before he had conducted some practical experiments. However, Soviet biologists are making serious attempts to harvest krill in the Antarctic and one of their research ships, using side trawls and pumps, succeeded in collecting 70 tons. But it was then found necessary to process the catch immediately (into "shrimp-meal" for animal feed) because even in the low Antarctic temperatures the krill spoiled within a few hours. Again, therefore, there are immense technical problems to be resolved, not only in the processing *in situ* and subsequent transporting of vast quantities of krill, but also in the cleaning and preparing for human consumption of a small crustacean, more than 25 per cent of which is shell. Technicians are so extraordinarily ingenious— terrifyingly so, in view of their apparent disregard for ecology —that it is conceivably possible that they may ultimately succeed in harvesting plankton and converting it into food for human consumption on a commercial scale. But then what is going to be the effect on the other inhabitants of the sea, all of whom are dependent directly or indirectly on the plankton for food? To fish for plankton commercially would be to embark blindly upon an operation that could change the entire ecological structure of the ocean and possibly result in the extinction of its main food potential, the fish and other sizeable fauna such as squids, octopuses and crabs.

It would be more sensible and also more practical to concentrate initially on conserving and building up existing stocks of fish, on extending the search for unexploited fishing grounds, and on making infinitely greater use of those species of fish that are at present regarded as inedible by Western peoples, and also of the astronomical numbers of squids and octopuses. There has been considerable research into the possibility of "farming" the sea, but experiments have not been encouraging. Increasing the stocks of fish by fertilizing the sea with minerals to stimulate the growth of planktonic food has not proved practicable, because the fertilizers are diluted and dispersed by currents; while their restricted use in bays and inlets partially protected from currents would not result in appreciable increases in the world's stock of fish and has in any case also proved impracticable.

If the fishing banks cannot be manured, can they be restocked from hatcheries? Again, experiments have not been encouraging. A high percentage of the larvae from hatchery eggs die, while 90 per cent of the fry may be undersized in comparison with wild fry and also abnormally colored. And as they are artificially bred and fed, they are not equipped to survive natural existence in the ocean. Moreover, it would probably never be feasible to transplant large enough numbers of young fish from hatcheries to add appreciably to the countless millions of fish already in the sea. One estimate, indeed, suggests that theoretically it would be necessary to transplant 20 million young plaice (as large and vigorous as wild stock) in a single year in order to increase the catch on a particular bank by 5 per cent four years later.

To all intents and purposes, therefore, we are thrown back on the conclusion that the only practical harvest to be won from the sea in the foreseeable future must be from existing stock of fish and other fauna. This harvest can certainly be increased substantially. For example, though many of the traditional banks have been overfished, there remain extensive areas that have hardly been touched by the commercial fishing fleets, notably the eastern sector of the North Pacific, the west coasts of South America and Africa, and parts of the Indian Ocean. Above all, it is a startling fact that the greater part of the oceans has never been fished, for we are only now beginning to discover that it is probably not the herrings and sardines of the upper waters that are the most numerous fish in the ocean, even though they are numbered in millions or billions, but those in the midwaters, of whose existence fishermen have hardly been aware—the lantern fish, the black scabbard fish, the deep-sea smelt *Bathylagus* and, perhaps more numerous than any of these, the bristle-mouths. These are all small fish, and new and revolutionary techniques will have to be devised for fishing at unprecedented depths; but if these virgin stocks could be harvested, the annual world catch of fish might be increased four- or five-fold to the substantial figure of 200 or 250 million tons.

It is true that a harvest of this order would feed only a small proportion of a vastly increased human population, but is the human population in fact going to continue increasing until it reaches saturation point? As a naturalist, I suspect that nature will devise a means of preventing such increase, just as she controls the cyclical rise and fall in the populations of other mammals such as lemmings and hares—providing, of course, that man does not forestall her by the deliberate or accidental dissemination of bacteria or nuclear radiation.

Appendix

SOME OF THE FISH, MAMMALS AND
INVERTEBRATES OF THE
ATLANTIC AND PACIFIC OCEANS

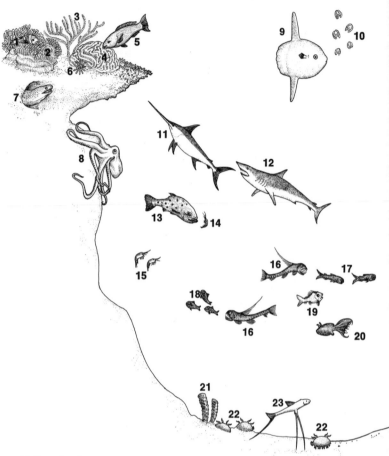

1. Yellow-faced anemone fish
2. Giant sea anemone
3. Gorgonian coral
4. Brain coral
5. Pink parrot fish
6. Slate-pencil urchin
7. Moray eel
8. Common octopus
9. Ocean sunfish
10. Comb jellyfish
11. Swordfish
12. Mako shark
13. Giant sea bass
14. Krill
15. Crimson deep sea prawns
16. Pacific viperfish
17. Lantern fish (*Myctophum spinosum*)
18. Lantern fish (*Electrena rissoi*)
19. Hatchet fish
20. *Vampiroteuthis infernalis*
21. Venus flower basket, glass sponge
22. Sea cucumber, two half-buried in bottom mud and a third walking
23. Tripod fish

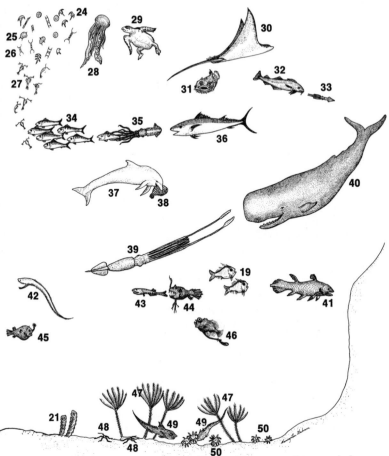

Plankton:

24. Dinoflagellates, *Ceratium*
25. Dinoflagellates, *Peridinium*
26. Diatoms
27. Copepods, *Calanus*
28. Jellyfish
29. Hawksbill turtle
30. Spotted eagle ray
31. Toadfish

32. Atlantic cod
33. Squid
34. Atlantic mackerel
35. Squid
36. Bluefin tuna
37. Bottle-nosed dolphin (*Tursiops truncatus*)
38. Naked sole
39. Giant squid (*Architeuthis*)

40. Sperm whale
41. Coelacanth
42. Gulper, or pelican fish
43. Bristlemouth
44. Deep-sea angler
45. Deep-sea angler
46. Kasidoron Edom
47. Sea lily
48. Brittle stars
49. The rattail
50. Anemones

Selected Bibliography

Aldrich, Herbert L. *Arctic Alaska and Siberia: or, Eight Months with the Arctic Whalemen.* Chicago and New York: Rand McNally & Company, 1889.

Alpers, Anthony. *Dolphins: The Myth and the Mammal.* Boston: Houghton Mifflin Company, 1961. London: John Murray Publishers, Ltd., 1963.

Bardach, John E. *Harvest of the Sea.* New York: Harper & Row, Publishers, 1968.

Barton, Otis. *Adventure: On Land and Under the Sea.* New York: Thomas Y. Crowell Company, 1953. London: Longmans, Green & Co., Ltd., 1954.

Bates, Marston. *Animal Worlds.* New York: Random House, 1963. London: Thomas Nelson & Sons, 1963.

Beebe, Charles William. *The Arcturus Adventure.* New York and London: G. P. Putnam's Sons, 1926.

——. *Galapagos: World's End.* New York and London: G. P. Putnam's Sons, 1924.

——. *Half-Mile Down.* New York: Harcourt, Brace & Co., 1934.

——. *Zaca Venture.* New York: Harcourt, Brace & Co., 1938.

Berrill, Norman John. *The Life of the Ocean.* New York: McGraw-Hill, Inc., 1966.

268

Brown, David H. and Norris, Kenneth S. "Observations of Captive Wild Cetaceans." *Journal of Mammalogy* 37 (1956): 311–326.

Bruun, Anton Frederik, ed. *The Galathea Deep-sea Expedition 1950–2: Described by Members of the Expedition.* New York: The Macmillan Company, 1956.

Budker, Paul. *Whales and Whaling.* New York: The Macmillan Company, 1958. London: George G. Harrap & Company, Ltd., 1958.

Carr, Archie Fairly. *The Turtle: A Natural History of Sea Turtles.* London: Cassell and Company, Ltd., 1968.

——. *The Windward Road: Adventures of a Naturalist on Remote Caribbean Shores.* New York: Alfred A. Knopf, Inc. 1955. London: Robert Hale & Company, 1957.

Carson, Rachel. *The Sea Around Us.* Rev. ed. New York: Oxford University Press, 1965.

Chapin, Henry and Smith, F. G. Walton. *The Ocean River.* New York: Charles Scribner's Sons, 1952.

Clarke, Robert. "Sperm Whales of the Azores." *Discovery*, 28 (1956): 239–298.

Coker, Robert Erwin. *This Great and Wide Sea: An Introduction to Oceanography and Marine Biology.* New York: Harper & Row Publishers, 1962.

Constantin-Weyer, Maurice. *The Private Life of Fishes.* Translated by Ray Turrel. London: Richard Bell Publishers, 1956.

Cousteau, Jacques-Yves. *The Silent World.* New York: Harper & Row, Publishers, 1953. London: Hamish Hamilton, Ltd., 1953.

——. *World Without Sun.* New York: Harper & Row, Publishers, 1965. London: William Heinemann, Ltd., 1965.

Cousteau, Jacques-Yves and Dugan, James. *The Living Sea.* New York: Harper & Row, Publishers, 1963. London: Hamish Hamilton, Ltd., 1963.

Cromie, William T. *Exploring the Secrets of the Sea.* Englewood Cliffs, N.J.: Prentice-Hall, Inc., 1962.

Davies, David Herbert. *About Sharks and Shark Attacks.* New York: Hobbs, Dorman & Co., 1966. London: Routledge & Kegan Paul, Ltd., 1965.

Diolé, Phillippe. *The Undersea Adventure.* Translated by Alan Ross. New York: Julian Messner, Inc., 1953. London: Sidgwick & Jackson, Ltd., 1953.

Doukan, Gilbert. *The World Beneath the Waves.* Translated by A. and

R. M. Case. New York: John DeGraff, Inc., 1958. London: George Allen & Unwin, Ltd., 1957.

Eibl-Eibesfeldt, Irenäus. *Land of a Thousand Atolls: A Study of Marine Life in the Maldive and Nicobar Islands.* Translated by Gwynne Vevers. Cleveland: The World Publishing Company, 1965. London: MacGibbon & Kee, Ltd., 1965.

Fraser, James. *Nature Adrift: The Story of Marine Plankton.* Philadelphia: Dufour Editions, 1962. London: G. T. Foulis & Co., 1962.

Gotto, R. V. *Marine Animals—Partnerships and Other Associations.* New York: American Elsevier Publishing Company, Inc., 1969. London: English Universities Press, 1969.

Gray, William Bittle. *Creatures of the Sea.* New York: Wilfred Funk, Inc., 1960.

Greenwood, Michael. "The Diver's Best Friend." *Animals* 10 (1967): 348–353.

Grimble, Sir Arthur. *A Pattern of Islands.* London: John Murray Publishers, Ltd., 1960.

Grønningsaeter, Arne. "Sjoørmen-Blekkspruten." *Naturen* 70 (1946): 379–380.

Günther, Klaus and Deckert, Kurt. *Creatures of the Deep Sea.* Translated by E. W. Dickes. New York: Charles Scribner's Sons, 1956. London: George Allen & Unwin, Ltd., 1956.

Harden-Jones, Frederick Robert. *Fish Migration.* New York: St. Martin's Press, 1968. London: Edward Arnold, Ltd., 1968.

Hardy, Sir Alister Clavering. *Great Waters: A Voyage of Natural History to Study Whales, Plankton and the Waters of the Southern Ocean.* New York: Harper & Row, Publishers, 1967. London: William Collins' Sons, 1967.

———. *The Open Sea—Its Natural History:* Part I, *The World of Plankton;* Part 2, *Fish and Fisheries.* Boston: Houghton Mifflin Company, 1959. London: William Collins' Sons, 1959.

Hass, Hans. *Diving to Adventure: Harpoon and Camera Under the Sea.* Translated by Barrows Mussey. London: Jarrolds & Sons, Ltd., 1956.

———. *Expedition Into the Unknown.* Translated by Gwynne Edwards. London: Hutchinson Publishing Group, Ltd., 1965.

———. *I Photographed Under the Seven Seas.* Translated by James Cleugh. London: Jarrolds & Sons, Ltd., 1956.

———. *Under the Red Sea with Spear and Camera.* Translated by James

Cleugh. New York: Rand McNally & Company, 1952. London: Jarrolds & Sons, Ltd., 1952.

——. *We Come From the Sea*. Translated by Alan Houghton Brodrick. Garden City, N.Y.: Doubleday & Company, Inc., 1959. London: Jarrolds & Sons, Ltd., 1958.

Heezen, B. C. "Whales Entangled in Deep Sea Cables." *Deep-Sea Research* 4 (1957): 105–115.

Herald, Earl Stannard. *Living Fishes of the World*. Garden City, N.Y.: Doubleday & Company, Inc., 1962. London: Hamish Hamilton, Ltd., 1961.

Heuvelmans, Bernard. *In the Wake of the Sea-Serpents*. Translated by Richard Garnett. New York: Hill & Wang, Inc., 1968. London: Rupert Hart-Davis, Ltd., 1968.

Heyerdahl, Thor. *Kon-Tiki: Across the Pacific by Raft*. Translated by F. H. Lyon. New York: Rand McNally & Company, 1964.

Hill, Ralph Nading. *Windows in the Sea*. New York: Holt, Rinehart and Winston, Inc., 1956. London: Victor Gollancz, Ltd., 1956.

Houot, Georges and Willm, Pierre. *2000 Fathoms Down*. Translated by Michael Bullock. New York: E. P. Dutton & Co., Inc., 1955. London: Hamish Hamilton, Ltd., 1955.

Idyll, Clarence P. *Abyss, the Deep Sea and the Creatures that Live in It*. New York: Thomas Y. Crowell Company, 1964.

——. *The Sea Against Hunger*. New York: Thomas Y. Crowell Company, 1970.

Jones, John Williams. *The Salmon*. London: William Collins' Sons, 1959.

Klingel, Gilbert. *Inagua: Which is the Name of a Very Lonely and Nearly Forgotten Island*. New York: Dodd, Mead & Company, 1940. London: Robert Hale & Company, 1942.

Lane, Frank Walter. *The Kingdom of the Octopus: The Life History of the Cephalopoda*. New York: Sheridan House, Inc., 1960. London: Jarrolds & Sons, Ltd., 1957.

Latil, Pierre de. *The Underwater Naturalist*. Translated by Edward Fitzgerald. Boston: Houghton Mifflin Company, 1954.

Lilly, John C. *Man and Dolphin*. Garden City, N.Y.: Doubleday & Company, Inc., 1961.

Lineaweaver, Thomas H. and Backus, Richard H. *The Natural History of Sharks*. Philadelphia: J. B. Lippincott Company, 1970.

McCormick, Harold W. and Allen, Tom. *Shadows in the Sea: The Sharks, Skates and Rays*. Philadelphia: Chilton Book Co., 1963.

MacGinitie, George Eber and MacGinitie, Nettie. *Natural History of Marine Animals*. 2d ed. New York: McGraw-Hill, Inc., 1968.

Marshall, Norman Bertram. *Aspects of Deep Sea Biology*. New York: Philosophical Library, 1954. London: Hutchinson's Scientific and Technical Publications, 1954.

——. *Life of Fishes*. Cleveland: The World Publishing Company, 1966. London: George Weidenfeld & Nicolson, Ltd., 1966.

Matthews, L. Harrison. "The Shark That Hibernates." *New Scientist* 13 (1962): 756–759.

Maxwell, Gavin. *Harpoon Venture*. New York: The Viking Press, Inc., 1952. London: Rupert Hart-Davis, Ltd., 1952.

Murphy, Robert Cushman. "Among the Pearl Islands: The Second Instalment in the Story of the 'Askoy' Expedition." *Natural History* 53 (1944): 274–281.
. "Beyond the Continental Shelf: The Third Installment in the 'Askoy' Expedition." *Natural History* 53 (1944): 303–309.

——. "The Coast of Winter Drought: Explorations in Northwestern South America—Chapter V of the Voyage of the Schooner 'Askoy'." *Natural History* 53 (1944): 398–406/430.

——. *Logbook for Grace: Whaling Brig Daisy*. New York: The Macmillan Company, 1947.

——. "Mountain and Sea in the Choco: The Sixth Installment in the Story of the 'Askoy' Expedition." *Natural History* 53 (1944): 474–481.

——. *Oceanic Birds of South America*. 2 vols. New York: The Macmillan Company and The American Museum of Natural History, 1948.

——. "To the Choco in the Schooner 'Askoy': Exploring One of the Least Known Coasts in the World." *Natural History* 53 (1944): 200–208.

——. "Wet Lands and Dry Seas: To the Choco in the Schooner 'Askoy', Chapter IV." *Natural History* 53 (1944): 350–356.

Murray, John and Hjort, Johan. *The Depths of the Ocean*. New York: Stechert-Hafner Service Agency, 1964.

Nicol, J. A. C. "Luminous Creatures of the Sea." *Sea Frontiers* 10 (1964): 143–154.

Nikol'skii, Georgii Vasil'evich. *The Ecology of Fishes*. Translated by L. Birkett. New York and London: Academic Press, Inc., 1963.

Norman, John Roxbrough. *A History of Fishes*. 2d ed. New York: Hill & Wang, Inc., 1963. London: Ernest Benn, Ltd., 1963.

Norman, John Roxbrough and Fraser, F. C. *Giant Fishes, Whales and Dolphins*. London: G. P. Putnam's Sons, 1937.

Norris, Kenneth S., ed. *Whales, Dolphins and Porpoises*. Berkeley: University of California Press, 1966.

Ommanney, Francis D. *A Draught of Fishes*. 2d ed. New York: Thomas Y. Crowell Company, 1966. London: Longmans, Green & Co., Ltd., 1965.

——. *The Ocean*. 2d ed. New York and London: Oxford University Press, 1961.

Parsons, James Jerome. *The Green Turtle and Man*. Gainesville, Fla.: University of Florida Press, 1962.

Perry, Richard. *Shetland Sanctuary: Birds on the Isle of Noss*. London: Faber & Faber, Ltd., 1948.

Piccard, Jacques and Dietz, Robert S. *Seven Miles Down: The Story of Bathyscaph Trieste*. New York: G. P. Putnam's Sons, 1961.

Pincher, Chapman. *A Study of Fish*. New York: Duell, Sloan & Pearce, Inc., 1948. London: Herbert Jenkins, Ltd., 1948.

Ray, Carleton and Ciampi, Elgin. *Underwater Guide to Marine Life*. Cranbury, N.J.: Barnes & Company, 1956. London: Nicholas Kaye, Ltd., 1958.

Riedman, Sarah Regal and Gustafson, Elton T. *Focus on Sharks*. New York: Abelard-Schuman Limited, 1969.

Robertson, Robert Blackwood. *Of Whales and Men*. New York: Alfred A. Knopf, Inc., 1954.

Robin, M-P. "Combat de Monstres." *Le Chasseur Francais* (November 1952).

Sanderson, Ivan Terence. *Follow the Whale*. Boston: Little, Brown & Company, 1956. London: Cassell & Company, Ltd., 1958.

Schroeder, Robert E. *Something Rich and Strange*. New York: Harper & Row, Publishers, 1965. London: George Allen & Unwin, Ltd., 1967.

Slijper, Everhard Johannes. *Whales*. Translated by A. J. Pomerans. New York: Basic Books, Inc., 1962. London: Hutchinson Publishing Group, Ltd., 1962.

Springer, Stewart. "Some Observations on the Behavior of Schools of Fishes in the Gulf of Mexico and Adjacent Waters." *Ecology* 39 (1957): 166–171.

Starkey, J. D. "I Saw a Sea Monster." *Animals* 2 (1964).

Stenuit, Robert. *The Dolphin, Cousin to Man*. Translated by Catherine Osborne. New York: Sterling Publishing Co., Inc., 1968.

Tucker, Denys W. "A New Solution to the Atlantic Eel Problem." *Nature* 183 (1959): 495–501.

Tweedie, Michael. "The Largest Fish of All Time." *Animals* 10 (1967): 258–259.

Walford, Lionel Albert. *Living Resources of the Sea: Opportunities for Research and Expansion.* New York: Ronald Press Co., 1958.

Winn, Howard E. "Communication by Marine Animals." *Oceanology International* 2 (1967): 32–34.

Index

275

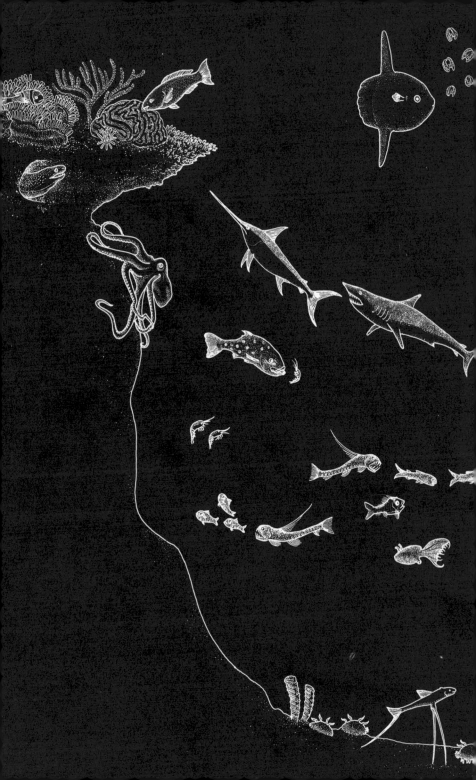